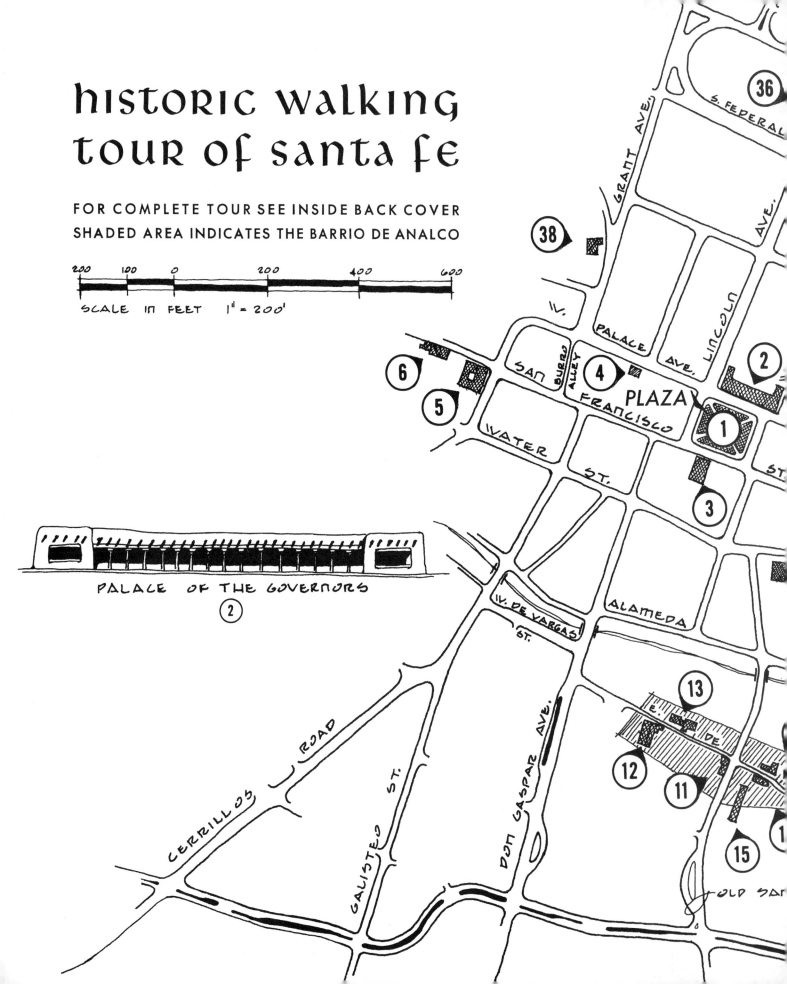

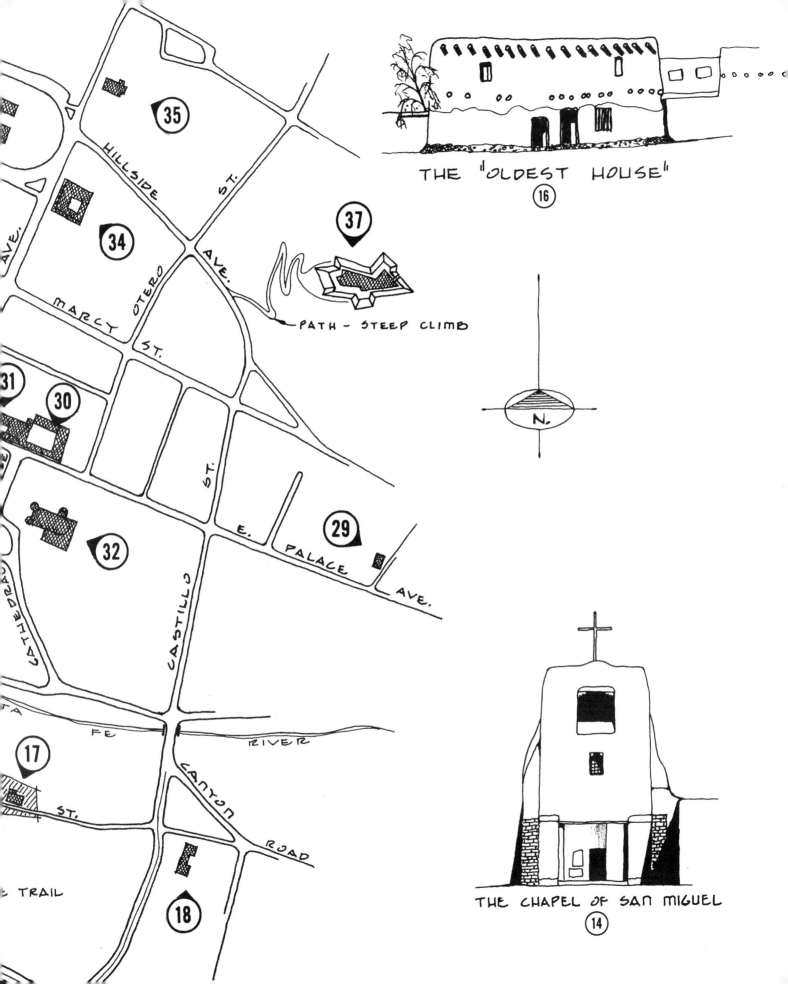

THE "OLDEST HOUSE"
16

PATH - STEEP CLIMB

N.

THE CHAPEL OF SAN MIGUEL
14

OLD SANTA FE TODAY

OLD SANTA FE TODAY

PREFACE BY JOHN GAW MEEM

Published for THE HISTORIC SANTA FE FOUNDATION

by UNIVERSITY OF NEW MEXICO PRESS *Albuquerque*

ACKNOWLEDGMENTS

To *The New Mexican* for permission to use certain portions of its copyrighted series "Let's Keep Our Heritage."

To the State of New Mexico Records Center for the assistance of the staff of its Division of Historical Services and its archival facilities.

To the Museum of New Mexico for the assistance of its research personnel and staff photographer.

To the Avery-Bowman Abstract Company and the Santa Fe Abstract and Title Company Incorporated for research assistance and use of property records.

To the owners of historic homes and buildings in Santa Fe who have permitted the structures included in this book to be photographed and described.

PHOTO CREDITS

Len Bouché—38
Ray Cary—75
Peter Dechert—front cover, 2, 19, 55, 60
James B. DeKorne—17, 18, 20, 25, 26, 27, 30, 32, 40, 53, 61, 72, 73
Tyler Dingee—back cover
Laura Gilpin—38, 48, 52, 54, 56, 77
Walter Goodwin—76
Karl Kernberger—9, 10, 12, 14, 16, 22, 31, 33, 34, 36, 41, 43, 49, 53, 63, 64, 66, 70, 78
Tony Perry—27 (right), 35, 37, 57
Ken Schar—44, 45, 62
Alan K. Stoker—23, 24, 28, 29, 35, 39, 42, 43, 46, 47, 50, 51, 52
Todd Webb—55, 68
Charlotte White—74
The following are from the files of the HSFF, photographers unknown—21, 33, 37, 58, 59

Manufactured in the U.S.A. by the University of New Mexico Printing Plant. Designed by Helen Gentry
Library of Congress Catalog Card No. 72-86822. International Standard Book Number 0-8263-0251-3
First edition 1966. Second edition, revised and enlarged, 1972; second printing 1975

PREFACE

THIS BOOK had its origin in a small pamphlet published by the Historic Santa Fe Foundation in 1962 entitled *Historic Buildings & Sites of Santa Fe.* Some of the material was later expanded into a series of articles, "Let's Keep Our Heritage," which appeared from time to time in *The New Mexican,* the local newspaper which has consistently backed the movement for the preservation of Santa Fe's historical assets. The series was edited by me and sponsored by the Old Santa Fe Association, with documentation furnished by the Historic Santa Fe Foundation.

These two organizations are at the heart of the movement for preserving the city's cultural heritage of historic and architecturally significant buildings. It is appropriate, however, to note that it was due to the generosity and foresight of historically minded citizens in former years that Santa Fe still has SENA PLAZA, restored by Miss Amelia E. White and others; the ARIAS DE QUIROS buildings, preserved by Mrs. William B. Field; and EL ZAGUAN and the BORREGO HOUSE, preserved by Mrs. Charles H. Dietrich.

The Old Santa Fe Association is the older organization, founded in 1926 with the avowed objective:

To preserve and maintain the ancient landmarks, historical structures, and traditions of Old Santa Fe, to guide its growth and development in such a way as to sacrifice as little as possible of that unique charm, born of age, tradition and environment which are the priceless assets and heritage of Old Santa Fe.

It has been at the forefront of every fight for conservation since then. Sometimes it has lost, as in the case of the Nusbaum Building, a fine example of Territorial architecture which was torn down by the city to make way for a parking lot, and the Curry House at the west end of the BARRIO DE ANALCO, which was demolished as a result of the Urban Renewal project.

But the association has often won, notably in its fight for the adoption of the city's Historic Zoning Ordinance, which protects the distinctive character of the historic area of Santa Fe by requiring that new construction harmonize with the old. This ordinance was drawn up by the Hon. Samuel Z. Montoya, at the time Santa Fe city attorney, now justice of the state supreme court, and members of the city planning commission Irene von Horvath and the late Oliver LaFarge. In a landmark victory in the struggle for historic preservation, the ordinance has been declared constitutional by the state supreme court.

The Historic Santa Fe Foundation was founded in 1961 to receive tax exempt donations, to administer property, and to engage in educational and research activities. Since then it has placed bronze plaques on 29 buildings in Santa Fe and its environs which as the result of its documented research were deemed worthy of preservation. In addition, it played an important role in having most of these (as well as others) placed on the State Register of Cultural Properties, from which several have been selected for designation as National Historic Landmarks. The Historic Santa Fe Foundation is currently administering, through a contractual agreement with the owner, the LORETTO CHAPEL, one of the properties it worked diligently to help preserve.

A tax-exempt organization such as the Historic Santa Fe Association is needed because gifts, both large and small, are required to save endangered historic and other significant buildings from destruction; and because the Old Santa Fe Association frequently must work to influence legislation on behalf of its objectives, it cannot receive or participate in tax-exempt donations.

The buildings and sites chosen for inclusion in both the original publication and in this revised and expanded edition were selected by the Board of Directors of the Historic Santa Fe Foundation as recommended by members of its Historic Research Committee. Those responsible for the research and writing of the texts for the items in this book include: Mrs. Lief Ericson Mueller, researcher; Mrs. Gertrude Hill Muir, formerly Librarian of the Museum of New Mexico, now a member of the Library staff of Arizona State University, Tempe, Arizona; Mrs. Sylvia G. Loomis, formerly Executive Secretary for both the Historic Santa Fe Foundation and the Old Santa Fe Association, now on the staff of the Archives of American Art, who edited the text of the first edition; J. D. Sena, Jr., and Boyd Cockrell of the Santa Fe Abstract and Title Company, Inc.; Bruce T. Ellis, former Curator of History of the Museum of New Mexico; Alan C. Vedder, Conservator for the Museum of New Mexico; E. Boyd, Curator Emeritus of the Spanish Colonial Arts Department of the Museum of New Mexico, and Myra Ellen Jenkins, State Historian and member of the staff of the New Mexico State Records Center, who was also responsible for the editing of this edition.

Publication of *Old Santa Fe Today* has been supported by the School of American Research. Founded in 1907 and quartered in Santa Fe since 1909, the school has a distinguished record of achievement in field archeology and anthropological research. Its participation in the 1912 remodeling of the PALACE OF THE GOVERNORS helped to establish the local regional style: the long portal on the PLAZA was reconstructed in a manner authentic to the traditions of the Santa Fe area. The school has conducted archeological excavations at such major southwestern sites as Chaco Canyon and Bandelier National Monument, and its four-year archeological project within and on the North Rim of the Grand Canyon in 1967-70 was the first systematic inquiry into early man's occupation and use of this great natural land feature. Its many scholarly professional seminars continue to bring credit to the Santa Fe community. The Board of the Historic Santa Fe Foundation acknowledges with appreciation the action of the Board of Managers of the School of American Research in making possible the inclusion of *Old Santa Fe Today* among the many distinguished publications in the school's long history.

The coordination between the Historic Santa Fe Foundation and the School of American Research has been under the direction of Milton R. Adler, immediate past chairman of the foundation and one of its founders. Dr. Peter Dechert, former Assistant Director of the School of American Research, has assisted in all matters concerning this publication.

The entire project has been one of cooperation on the part of many individuals, devoted to the task of recording and preserving the architecture, traditions and history of Old Santa Fe. It is their hope that this book will move others to help Santa Fe keep its character and individuality by supporting the organizations dedicated to this purpose.

John Gaw Meem

CONTENTS

⊖ Indicates that the Historic Santa Fe Foundation has placed a bronze plaque on this building to designate it as being worthy of preservation.

SANTA FE'S
INDIGENOUS ARCHITECTURE

A BRIEF account of the origin and development of Santa Fe's distinctive architectural styles may help the reader who is unfamiliar with this region to a greater enjoyment of this book. There are two principal styles: the Spanish Pueblo and the Territorial.

The Spanish Pueblo, as the name implies, is a style derived from the mixture of Spanish architecture brought in by the Spanish colonizers and that of the Pueblo Indians of the Rio Grande Valley in which Santa Fe is located. The Pueblos, long before Columbus discovered America, had developed traditional forms and techniques of construction admirably suited to this arid country. It is not surprising therefore that the Spaniards, who also came from an arid land, should have adopted the essence of the Indian construction.

This consisted of a unit or room which the Indians combined in many ways to form pueblos, or apartment houses, for communal living and mutual defense. This unit was an approximately rectangular room with stone or puddled adobe walls, an earth floor, and a flat roof. The roof was supported by pine logs, or *vigas,* cut in the nearby forests and laid on top of the walls, about 30 inches apart. These in turn were covered with small poles or slats close to each other at right angles or diagonally to the *vigas.* Next came a bed of brush or weeds on which earth was tamped and graded to drain the water into wooden spouts in the parapets that surmounted the walls.

Virtually all of the above features were utilized by the Spanish colonists, and indeed most are in use to the present day. The flat room, then, coming down from time immemorial, is the principal characteristic of the Spanish Pueblo style. To this must be added the preponderance of unbroken wall surfaces in relation to door and window openings. This was due to the need to conserve heat in the winter and to keep it out in the summer, and also for defense against enemies.

A complete account of this style, for which space

is not available here, would take into account the variations in plan brought from Spain, one of the most prevalent being the house built around an inner *patio,* surrounded with *portales,* or porches, similar to the way in which Indian pueblo dwellings surround a large central plaza. Santa Fe was full of such houses in the 19th century, including those still to be found in the ARIAS DE QUIROS site. Greater detail would also be needed to describe the monumental flat-roofed missions built by the Franciscan friars who came here with the soldiers and colonists. These stone or adobe churches were built with the help of Indian labor, but their techniques were supplemented by Spanish tools and know-how. With these, they shaped logs into richly carved ceiling beams and fashioned elaborate capitals and bolsters, which trace their origin to Moorish Spain, as well as ornamental grilles and doors. Some of these items found their way into civic and domestic architecture. But in general, and to summarize, the exterior of an average house in the Spanish Pueblo style would be of adobe, rectangular in shape, with a flat roof surrounded by a low parapet, and soft in outline owing to hand construction and erosion; there would be few doors and windows in relation to the wall surfaces.

Santa Fe still has hundreds of such houses—modified through the intervening years—which, while not important enough to be designated as significant or historic buildings, nevertheless contribute to the overall character of the city. They constitute the main ingredient of Santa Fe's "collective facade."

With the opening of the Santa Fe Trail and the occupation by the American army in 1846, a new style developed, based on the ancient flat-roofed forms of the Spanish Pueblo but strongly modified by new techniques and new materials brought over the trail. Because its development coincided roughly with the period during which New Mexico was a territory, it has been called the Territorial style. Shortly after the arrival of the Americans, hard-burned brick was produced locally, and almost the first use to which it was put was to protect the exposed adobe parapets (adobe gradually dissolves and crumbles when exposed to rain and wind) by covering the tops with a few layers of brick, often in decorative patterns. This has become almost the symbol of the Santa Fe Territorial style. It recalls continuity with the ancient forms, based on the flat roof, whereas Territorial buildings with pitched roofs are hardly distinguishable from the style developed in California and elsewhere under the influence of the American occupation.

The old handmade windows were replaced with mill-made ones with double hung sash. Millwork was brought in to trim the doors and windows which reflected the current Greek Revival styles in St. Louis and Kansas, and was copied locally in a naive and attractive manner. The round posts around the patios and across the facades, with their carved bolster capitals, or corbels, were replaced with slender rectangular columns. Much of the new woodwork was painted. Perhaps the most drastic innovation was the covering of the walls with lime and later cement stucco to protect them against erosion. In the old days the maintenance of adobe plaster was done by women, but with changing customs this was no longer the case, and it became too expensive to hire help for this purpose. While the stucco has introduced a harder line and texture than the soft outlines of adobe, it has nevertheless proved to be important; without it many old buildings might not have survived.

There is still a third classification possible for Santa Fe buildings, which reflects the styles of the outside world rather than local regional conditions. Typical are the CATHEDRAL OF ST. FRANCIS and the UNITED STATES COURT HOUSE. To preserve Santa Fe's unique Pueblo-Territorial heritage, however, the city's Historic Zoning Ordinance now prohibits buildings designed in other styles from being erected within the historic area.

BARN OF JACAL CONSTRUCTION
(JUAN JOSE PRADA HOUSE, PAGE 39)

LA VILLA DE SANTA FE

IN THE WINTER OF 1609-10, 10 years before the Pilgrims landed at Plymouth Rock, the Villa of Santa Fe was founded as the seat of government for the vast region of the Southwest, then under the rule of the viceroy of New Spain (Mexico). It has been the capital of New Mexico since that date, and is therefore the oldest capital city in the United States. Santa Fe still retains much of its original Spanish character.

Seventy years earlier, the northern Mexican frontier, including Arizona and New Mexico, had been explored by Francisco Vásquez de Coronado, the young governor of the province of Nueva Vizcaya. In 1598, the first Spanish settlement in this region was established by Don Juan de Oñate on the east side of the Rio Grande near San Juan Pueblo; it was relocated across the river in 1599. The colony was moved to the site of Santa Fe in 1610 by Governor Pedro de Peralta, acting under orders from the viceroy to found a new capital.

There is archeological evidence that portions of Santa Fe were built on the site of an early Indian pueblo known as *Kuapoge,* or "place of shell beads near the water," but this prehistoric ruin was obliterated by the time the Spaniards arrived.

Throughout the 200 years of Spanish rule which followed its establishment, the walled city of Santa Fe was headquarters for political administration as well as for further exploration and missionary work among the Indians. Its only supply line was the Camino Real ("royal road"), stretching hundreds of miles south by caravan and horseback to Chihuahua and Mexico City, through arid, hostile country. Until the successful revolt of Mexico from Spain in 1821, foreign explorers and traders were not welcome in the province of Nuevo Méjico, and in 1807, Lieutenant Zebulon Pike, for whom Pike's Peak was named, was brought here as a prisoner for trespassing on Spanish soil.

Within a few months of Mexican independence, however, William Becknell of Missouri was met by New Mexican troops south of the Raton Pass and encouraged to come to Santa Fe with the first load of U.S. trade goods, thereby opening the famous Santa Fe Trail. From that time until after occupation by the United States, the city served as the vital link between traders from the east and from Mexico.

At the beginning of war between Mexico and this country, the Department of New Mexico was annexed to the United States. On August 18, 1846, Brigadier General Stephen Watts Kearny, commander of the Army of the West, marched his troops into Santa Fe and raised the U.S. flag over the Palace of the Governors. In anticipation of trouble which never came, FORT MARCY was built on a hill northeast of the city, where its ruins remain as a symbol of America's Manifest Destiny of westward expansion to the Pacific.

PALACE OF THE GOVERNORS VIEWED FROM THE PLAZA (TEXT AND OTHER PICTURES ON PAGES 12–15)

1
THE PLAZA

ORIGINALLY OF RECTANGULAR shape and reaching east as far as the present Cathedral, the Plaza has always been the heart of Santa Fe. During the establishment of the city as a villa in 1610, it was laid out as the usual Spanish *plaza mayor,* designed for military and religious functions and therefore made "at least half again as long as its width, because this form is best for celebrations with horses." On the north side stood the *casas reales* or PALACE OF THE GOVERNORS, and on the other three were built the homes of prominent citizens. It served as the setting for daily markets, chicken pulls, cockfights and other social gatherings, as well as for the public stocks and flogging post. The town crier used it to make public proclamations.

The Plaza was the central scene for the Pueblo Revolt of 1680 in which the Indians successfully besieged the Spaniards barricaded within the Palace, then allowed them to retire to El Paso del Norte. General de Vargas triumphantly rode into it twice, once on the reconnoitering expedition of 1692, and again in 1693 to reconquer the Kingdom of New Mexico. Because the Indians had razed the buildings, except for the Palace, which they had fortified, Santa Fe was rebuilt.

Encroachment on the Plaza began at an early period although Governor Cruzat y Góngora had decreed that streets should be made and kept at the width of 8 *varas* (approximately 22 feet). In the 1740's, the governor bought a house in order to demolish it because it obstructed the entrance to the parish church. In 1756, Governor Marín del Valle ordered certain citizens to open the streets upon which they had encroached with fences and buildings, especially "in front of the house of this Royal Presidio." By 1800, however, the Plaza had been greatly reduced in size.

With Mexican independence from Spain in 1821, the Plaza was renamed the Plaza of the Constitution. In the late 1820's, a rock sundial was set up on a 9-foot adobe base in the center of the Plaza as "the only public clock to guide the authorities and employees." It bore the inscription: *Vita fugit sicut umbra* ("life flees like a shadow").

From 1821 to the arrival of the railroad, the Plaza was the end of the Santa Fe Trail, and caravans of Yankee merchandise were unloaded at the customs house on the east side. It was also the terminus for the Chihuahua trade which interlocked with that of the Santa Fe traders from the Missouri towns.

A bullring stood in the Plaza for a short time in 1844, but was torn down after Ute Indians made it their ambush to attack Governor Martínez de Lejanza in the Palace. In 1846, General Kearny proclaimed the annexation of New Mexico by the United States, with himself as military governor, to the citizens assembled in the Plaza.

For a few weeks in 1862, Confederate forces occupied Santa Fe, and their flag flew over the Plaza before their defeat at the battle of Glorieta forced them to retreat to Texas. The obelisk in the center of the Plaza commemorates New Mexico's defenders against both hostile Indian attack and Confederate invasion, and is probably the only monument to Union forces south of the Mason and Dixon line. In territorial days, the Plaza had a white picket fence around it and a gingerbread wooden bandstand where concerts were given by the Fort Marcy band.

The Plaza of Santa Fe was declared a National Historic Landmark in 1962. Since that year, the commercial buildings on its three sides, all erected within the past century, have been unified by *portales* over the facades.

2
PALACE OF THE GOVERNORS

THE PALACE OF THE GOVERNORS, constructed in 1610 following the establishment of the Villa of Santa Fe by Governor Pedro de Peralta, is the oldest public building in the United States which has been in continuous use. Originally, the royal houses and grounds ran from the Plaza north to the site of the present federal buildings and contained the governor's private apartments, official reception rooms and offices, military barracks, stables, arsenal, and servants' quarters. Vegetable gardens were planted in a central patio consisting of some 10 acres. The Palace extended farther to the west in Spanish times, and had two *torreones* or defense towers on the east and west corners of the facade. The western tower served as a prison and for storage of gunpowder. No *portal* existed.

During the Pueblo Revolt of 1680, the troops and refugees gathered within the Palace and resisted attacks until the Indians, after a 10-day siege, cut off the water supply and forced the Spaniards to retreat to the El Paso region. During the next 12 years, the Indians pulled down the houses and the parish church and used the adobe bricks to fortify the Palace. Upon his reconquest in 1693, General de Vargas found that the building had only one or two entrances, no outside windows, four or five defensive towers, and walls around the whole complex. Within, the Indians had subdivided the Spanish rooms into typical Indian cubicles with thin, puddled partitions, remains of which still exist in some interior walls.

Turning the tables on the rebels, de Vargas also cut off the water supply from the springs to the east and forced the Indians to surrender after some days of bloody attacks on the fortress. The governor, soldiers, colonists and priests all lived in the Palace until other housing could be provided. For want of a chapel, de Vargas had the Franciscans purify and bless the east *torreón,* which the Pueblos had made into a pagan *kiva.* When de Vargas died in 1704, there was still no principal church, and it is probable that he was buried in the floor of the *torreón* chapel, which then extended out into the Plaza and Washington Street. After the parish church was built in 1714, the *torreones* on the Palace were torn down in order to straighten the Plaza. When the southeastern room was excavated in 1965, the foundations of the east *torreón* were clearly visible, but no remains of de Vargas were found. His bones may still lie under the passing traffic of that busy street corner.

The Palace as the seat of government saw such distinguished incumbents as Marín del Valle, who built the military chapel with its stone altar screen, and Juan de Anza, who after founding the city of San Francisco in California was sent to New Mexico as governor and saved the province from near extermination at the hands of the Comanche. The visit of Bishop of Durango Pedro de Tamarón in 1760 was celebrated by a reception in the Palace and procession to the parish church. In 1807, Lieutenant Zebulon M. Pike was interrogated in the Palace after he and his few companions had been arrested on the headwaters of the Rio Grande.

Mexican governors continued to occupy the building for official business and private residence. At different times, rooms were used for different purposes; what was once a *sala,* or reception and ballroom, or perhaps a governor's apartment, was later a council room or library. On August 18, 1846, Brigadier General Stephen Watts Kearny occupied the Palace in the name of the United States. Confederate forces used it as headquarters for a few weeks in 1862.

In time, the Palace was outgrown and a territorial capitol was built across the Santa Fe River. This capitol was later burned and rebuilt. The original building was still used for offices, but was in such sad condition that the territorial government threatened to tear it down, only to be stopped by the protests of public-spirited citizens. The 1909 legislature appropriated funds to convert it into the Museum of New Mexico, and remodeling for this purpose was completed in 1913. The graceful, scroll-saw *portal* of 1878 was replaced by the present one of earlier Spanish style, but Victorian doors and windows were retained. The Palace exhibits include prehistoric archeology materials, as well as those from Spanish, Mexican, and United States periods.

In common with the Santa Fe Plaza, the Palace was designated a National Historic Landmark in 1961.

15

3 LA CASTRENSE

ONE OF THE FINEST 18th century New Mexico churches once stood on this site, according to the description of Bishop Tamarón, who made a visitation of Santa Fe during its construction in 1760, and the later account of Fr. Francisco Atanasio Domínguez in 1776. This was the chapel of Our Lady of Light, or La Castrense, the military chapel for the presidial company of Santa Fe.

La Castrense was erected at the expense of Governor Francisco Marín del Valle on land he had bought on the south side of the plaza. Artisans brought from Mexico by the governor carved the handsome *reredos,* or altar screen, from white stone quarried in the Jacona region north of Santa Fe. Special high masses were occasionally celebrated in La Castrense and *Te Deums* sung to commemorate victories in Indian campaigns. Among prominent persons buried in the chapel were Bernardo Miera y Pacheco and Francisco de Anza, brother of Governor Juan de Anza, both in 1785.

By 1835, the chapel was closed because the Mexican government no longer provided funds for chaplains. After 1846, when U.S. forces occupied the city, it was used as an ammunition storeroom, then refitted for use by the district court of the first judicial district. In August, 1851, former governor Donaciano Vigil protested against such secular use of a consecrated building. After some contention, the court was moved to the Palace of the Governors, and La Castrense was formally returned to Bishop Jean Baptiste Lamy. For several years it was again used as a place of worship.

In 1859 the bishop sold the east portion of the property to Levi Spiegelberg, and the following year he deeded the building and the remaining land to merchant Simon Delgado in exchange for "$2,000 to make repairs on the parroquia," plus a deed to Delgado's land near SAN MIGUEL CHAPEL, where Lamy wished to build a boys' school.

When La Castrense was sold in 1859, the carved stone *reredos* was carefully removed to the old *parroquia* and placed in the sanctuary. There it remained concealed by a wall after the present Cathedral was built in 1869-86. In 1940, it was installed in the new CHURCH OF CRISTO REY. Corbels and *vigas* from La Castrense were also placed in the GUADALUPE CHAPEL on Agua Fria Street.

During partial demolition in 1859, the north walls of the chapel were taken down. Shops and warehouses were built to a depth of 60 feet back from the present sidewalk, covering the small cemetery. Some of the remaining interior walls were still standing as late as 1955. Before they were torn down to make way for the present J. C. Penney store, the site was excavated and the walls measured and studied by the Laboratory of Anthropology of the Museum of New Mexico.

16

4 FELIPE B. DELGADO HOUSE

AN EXCELLENT EXAMPLE of local adobe construction modified by late 19th century architectural detail, this house was built in 1890 by Felipe B. Delgado, socially prominent Santa Fe merchant, and remained in possession of the Delgado family until 1970, when it was purchased and renovated by John Gaw Meem. The stone base was laid by masons who had helped to build ST. FRANCIS CATHEDRAL, and the balcony, window casings, and elaborate wooden trim show the same influence that caused the extensive remodeling of the PALACE OF THE GOVERNORS in the Victorian manner after the Civil War.

Don Felipe was a grandson of Captain Manuel Delgado, founder of the Delgado family in New Mexico, who enlisted in the Royal Army of Spain in 1776 and came to New Mexico in 1778. Many members of the family—including four brothers of Felipe —became merchants and were prominent in public life.

Felipe Delgado was educated in St. Louis, Missouri. Later he operated a general store in Santa Fe and was one of the principal owners of mule and ox trains freighting over the Santa Fe Trail to Independence and the Camino Real to Chihuahua. His wife was Doña Lucía Ortiz, daughter of another prominent citizen and trader, Captain Gaspar Ortiz y Alaríd, for whom Don Gaspar Avenue and Ortiz Street in Santa Fe are named.

In 1877, when Don Felipe bought the land on which this house now stands, it was part of the picket line for cavalry horses and wagon trains at the end of the Santa Fe Trail. During his lifetime the house was the scene of great social activity, typical of territorial days during the late 19th and early 20th centuries. He is buried in ROSARIO CEMETERY.

5, 6
THE ORTIZ HOUSES

306-308 AND 322½ WEST SAN FRANCISCO STREET

IN THE LATE 1700's, these two structures formed the eastern and western sections of the Santa Fe hacienda of Antonio José Ortiz, on property which extended south to present Water Street and westward beyond what is now Jefferson. The house at 322½ is the older portion and had been the residence of his father, Nicolás Ortiz III. It is clearly depicted on the Joseph de Urrutia map of 1766, which also shows the same street pattern for San Francisco that now exists. How much older than 1766 the Nicolás Ortiz house may be is not known, but its thick adobe walls are more than 200 years old.

The Ortiz family is one of the most famous "first families" of New Mexico. Nicolás I came with de

Vargas as a civilian colonist in 1693. His son, Nicolás II, was a military man and held important civil posts. Nicolás III, son of Nicolás II, was captain of the Santa Fe presidio when he was killed August 31, 1769, in a skirmish with the Comanche near San Antonio Mountain. When Governor Pedro Fermín de Mendinueta called upon Ortiz' widow, Josefa Bustamante, at her home to offer his condolences, she sadly remarked that such evils happened in New Mexico because there was "no sworn Patron Saint." The governor and the widow decided to hold a public celebration in honor of Our Lady of the Rosary, "La Conquistadora," for intercession to protect New Mexico from further Indian attack. The

18

celebration, held in 1770, is the first documented Santa Fe Fiesta since 1712, when the city council had decreed an annual fiesta in honor of the 20th anniversary of General de Vargas' first expedition to reconquer New Mexico.

In 1771, Nicolás' son, Antonio José, and five others formed a committee to perpetuate the program. By 1776, the fiesta was a three-day affair, beginning with vespers the preceding evening, followed by masses, religious processions, theatrical performances and games, with government officials in attendance at all events, escorted by the royal garrison firing salvos. Citizens set *luminarias* for the occasion. This description is very similar to today's Santa Fe Fiesta.

Antonio José Ortiz was one of the largest landowners in New Mexico, with ranches, including one at Pojoaque, and extensive grazing lands. An important trader between Santa Fe and Mexico, he maintained a 12-room dwelling at El Paso for the use of his family and agents on trading trips. He contributed to the building of OUR LADY OF GUADALUPE CHURCH and ROSARIO CHAPEL, the repair of SAN MIGUEL CHAPEL, La Conquistadora chapel, and the parish church of St. Francis.

Antonio José enlarged the original Santa Fe home to include the section at 306-308 West San Francisco. When completed, his residence contained 18 rooms, with galleries, stables, bakery and the Oratorio of San José. This family chapel, also open to the public, was recessed from the street and located within the portion of the house which lay between the two presently existing structures. The map of Santa Fe drawn by Lieutenant J. F. Gilmer in 1846 immediately following the occupation by the United States shows the entire building.

By 1855, the *oratorio* had fallen into disuse. In that year, the Ortiz family property came into the hands of Anastacio Sandoval, merchant, colonel in the New Mexico militia during and after the Civil War, territorial treasurer in 1864, auditor in 1867, adjutant general in 1871, and member of the territorial legislature for 16 years. The street which bears his name was apparently laid out shortly after the purchase, and he used the eastern section on the corner of San Francisco and the new street, built by Antonio José Ortiz, as headquarters for his large

mercantile establishment. In 1870, Sandoval conveyed this portion, which consisted then of 10 rooms, 2 *zaguanes,* a *placita* with *portales,* a corral on the south and *portales* on the east and west, to Pedro Aranda. This land subsequently changed hands several times.

The next year, 1871, Sandoval also sold the original Nicolás Ortiz house at 322½ West San Francisco. After a succession of owners, the older portion was purchased by the Abeytia family of Socorro in 1884, and has been in the possession of Abeytia descendants since that date.

Through changes of fortune and usage, the two buildings, once portions of Santa Fe's most imposing home, have fallen into less desirable status, but within their walls, especially those of the Nicolás Ortiz house, governors, bishops and military visitors were once entertained, New Mexico policies decided, and the Santa Fe Fiesta revived.

7

CHAPEL
OF OUR LADY OF GUADALUPE

ARCHIVES OF THE Archdiocese of Santa Fe show that a license to build this chapel was recorded on October 14, 1795. The date of its completion is uncertain, but it is probably the oldest shrine dedicated to the Virgin of Guadalupe that has survived in the United States. When first built, the chapel was typical of 18th century New Mexico, of adobe, cruciform, with a three-tiered tower, sand-cast copper bells and the large painting on canvas of the Virgin of Guadalupe, which is signed on both front and back: "Jose de Alzibar, 1783." Alzibar was a popular painter of New Spain.

Antonio José Ortiz, the richest man in Santa Fe, in his will of January 31, 1805, left 1,500 sheep with whose products the costs of the annual function of Our Lady of Guadalupe were to be paid. Ortiz and his wife may well have given the painting by Alzibar to the chapel when it was completed since Ortiz was a merchant who made frequent trips to Mexico.

When the military chapel, LA CASTRENSE, was dismantled, the *vigas* and corbels from it were taken to the Guadalupe chapel. Cores from them give a tree-ring date of 1753. In 1856, an itinerant bell-caster, Francisco Luján, cast a bell in front of the old Santa Fe parish church which was then placed in the tower of the Guadalupe chapel. This bell was later sold. Its inscription read:

JUAN SENA Y DA. MARIA MANUELA DE ATOCHA-SANTA FE AGOSTO 21 DE 1856.

Sena and his wife were the donors of the bell.

When the railroad arrived in 1880, Archbishop Lamy appointed Father de Fouri to be pastor for the newly arrived, non-Spanish-speaking Roman Catholics. Extensive remodeling in the neo-Gothic style took place on the interior, Gothic windows were cut in the walls, and a peaked shingle roof was added. In 1922 the church was again remodeled after a fire, this time in California mission style instead of that of Franciscan New Mexico. After a new church was built next to it in 1961, the old chapel was neglected until recently, but is now being repaired through efforts of members of the parish. The choir loft from LA CASTRENSE and the Alzibar painting, cleaned and restored in 1969 by Paraguayan scholar Dr. Estella Rodríguez Cubero, are still in place.

8
DONACIANO VIGIL HOUSE

518 ALTO STREET (OPEN FOR VISITORS IF SIGN IS DISPLAYED)

IN 1832, THIS HOUSE with its farm lands and orchard was the residence of minor city official Juan Cristóbal Vigil, his wife María Antonia Andrea Martínez, and his large family, among whom was a soldier son, Donaciano. It then apparently included the buildings on either side of the front portion, as Juan Cristóbal in his will dated May 31 of that year and María Antonia in her testament of May 26, 1834, described it as "composed of four parts." After the death of his mother, Donaciano bought out the other heirs and added still another section, probably on the south. Today, the buildings facing Alto Street have different owners, but the main part of the house, with its charming inner *placita,* is the private residence of the person responsible for its restoration. The doors and windows used in the restoration came from the original Loretto Academy in Santa Fe and are Territorial in style.

The house is of special historic value, in addition to its charm and antiquity, as the former residence of Donaciano Vigil, one of the most important military and political figures of his day. While Santa Fe was under Mexican rule, 1821 to 1846, he served first in the presidial company of Santa Fe and then commanded the company of San Miguel del Vado. He was also military secretary to Governor Manuel Armijo. After U.S. occupation in 1846, General Kearny appointed him secretary of the territory, and in January, 1847, he became acting civil governor of New Mexico following the assassination of Governor Charles Bent. From 1848 to 1850 he continued as secretary of the territory and register of land titles.

In 1851, Donaciano led the opposition to the secular use of LA CASTRENSE by the U.S. government. As a member of the Santa Fe grand jury, he refused to take his place in the courtroom of the U.S. court of the first judicial district which had been located by Judge Grafton Baker within the church, and his stand against violation of a consecrated structure where his own father was buried resulted in the removal of the court to the PALACE OF THE GOVERNORS. Some reports of the incident state that Judge Baker threatened to arrest Vigil, but changed his mind when the townspeople and army personnel rallied to Vigil's support.

When this house served as the home of Donaciano Vigil and his wife, Doña Refugia Sánchez, its lands extended along the Rio de Santa Fe and still contained the orchard mentioned in his parents' wills. At that time, it was the scene of much civic and political activity, but in 1855 the Vigils retired to their ranch on the Pecos River, and in 1856 sold the property to Vicente García. They are buried in ROSARIO CEMETERY.

24

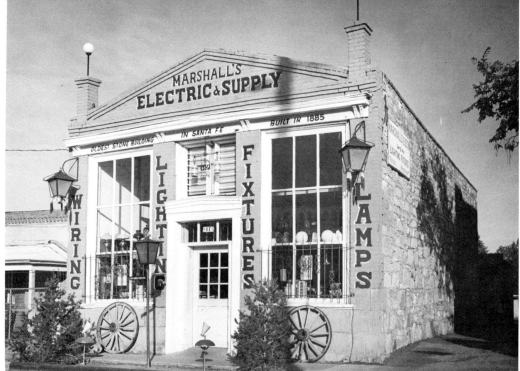

9
STONE STORE

316 GUADALUPE STREET

THIS BUILDING, erected about 1885, is probably the oldest stone commercial structure in Santa Fe. Originally constructed of rough, undressed stones to serve as a warehouse, the east side, which fronts on Guadalupe Street, was later faced with bricks and sandstone blocks to form a typical late 19th century mercantile facade.

The Saiz Store is located in the section south of the Santa Fe River designated during the late Spanish and Mexican periods as the Barrio de Guadalupe, since its residents were in the jurisdiction of the CHAPEL OF OUR LADY OF GUADALUPE.

This barrio, in common with the BARRIO DE ANALCO which joined it on the east, was the district inhabited by the common soldiers and their families. In 1860, the land on which the store is now located belonged to the Tapia family. Several Tapias had been soldiers in the presidial company of Santa Fe during the Mexican period, as had their neighbor, José Salaices, who owned much of the adjoining property. Salaices sold his holdings shortly thereafter, and the new owners and the Tapias built their houses along Agua Fria and present Guadalupe

streets so that they formed a complex within which was a *placita* common to the various landowners.

Cesaria Tapia sold the southern part of her property to Frederick Schnepple, a merchant and shopkeeper, in 1880. He apparently erected the stone building to serve as a warehouse before conveying the property to merchant John Dendahl on June 28, 1886, since the deed of that transaction contains the first direct reference to the building. It specifies the real property sold as including a frame dwelling, stable, sheds, an adobe residence, and a stone storehouse, and states that the property adjoined the common *placita*. The storehouse also appears on the 1886 Hartman map.

For several years prior to the sale of the property by Dendahl to Alphonse Dockwiler in 1916, the building was used as a brewery by Henry Krick, agent for Lemp's Key and Bottled Beer. Dockwiler owned the building for 10 years before conveying it in 1926 to J. A. Hart, who used it as headquarters for the Coca Cola Bottling Company. The structure, presently owned by Marshall Saiz, now houses Marshall's Electric and Supply Company.

25

10 HESCH HOUSE

324-326 READ STREET (PRIVATE RESIDENCE)

THIS TWO-STORY HOUSE was built in 1888 by Philip Hesch, a Canadian-born master carpenter of German extraction who had recently arrived in Santa Fe with his large family. Characterized by an imposing mansard roof and "carpenter style" exterior ornament, it is one of the few remaining late 19th century structures in the city influenced by contemporary European architectural details.

The abstract for the property begins with the conveyance of a parcel of land from Charles Lerouge and his wife, María Rita García, to John Allen on May 12, 1869. During the next 10 years, Allen and other buyers acquired much of the adjoining land for speculative purposes in anticipation of the construction of the Atchison, Topeka and Santa Fe Railroad spur from Lamy Junction. The addition thus assembled was originally designated as "Valuable Building Lots" on the Santa Fe city map of 1880, and the lots on which this house was built were numbered 258 and 259. This description of

26

the property has been repeated in all later transactions.

After passing through several hands, the property was purchased from Annie H. Hull by Hesch on March 19, 1888, and construction was soon started on the house which was to serve as the family home for many years. In 1906, Philip Hesch deeded the house to his wife, Catherine, "in love and affection." Six years later, the property was sold to Arthur G. Whittier, and Mr. and Mrs. Hesch moved to California. Some of their descendants, however, still live in Santa Fe. The property has changed hands several times since 1912 and is now owned by Mr. and Mrs. Eloy Ulibarri.

The house is of frame construction, and originally the second story was shingled. In recent years, however, the exterior has been completely stuccoed. The interior on the east side has been remodeled, but the western portion, which contains a handsome carved wooden staircase (opposite) and much of the original woodwork, remains as it was built.

11 BARRIO DE ANALCO

THIS *BARRIO* OR district, in the center of which is the CHAPEL OF SAN MIGUEL, is the oldest settlement of European origin in Santa Fe except for the Plaza, and hence one of the oldest in the United States. Originally settled in the 1600's by Tlaxcalan Indian servants from Mexico who came with the Franciscan missionaries and Spanish officials, it took the Nahuatl word *analco* ("the other side of the water") to distinguish it from the Plaza area, which was on the north side of the Rio de Santa Fe. Soon after the Barrio de Analco was settled, the original CHAPEL OF SAN MIGUEL was built to serve as the mission church.

During the Pueblo Revolt of 1680, the Barrio de Analco was the first section of Santa Fe to be sacked and razed by attackers from "all the Tanos and Pecos nations, and the Querez of San Marcos armed and giving war-whoops." The rebels approached through the cultivated fields to the south. Those residents who escaped took refuge in the PALACE OF THE GOVERNORS with the beleaguered Spaniards and later retreated with Governor Otermín to El Paso. After the reconquest, only a few of its former settlers returned, but the Barrio was soon rebuilt by others.

By 1776 the Barrio de Analco was occupied by married soldiers, *genízaro* servants (Indians living in a Europeanized status), and other laborers. It is probable that some buildings still standing in this area were built before that date.

Several buildings described on the following pages are located within the Barrio de Analco. This concentration of structures, deemed worthy of preservation from both historical and architectural standpoints, provides an authentic setting for the CHAPEL OF SAN MIGUEL and points up the significance and importance of the Barrio to Santa Fe.

12
ROQUE TUDESQUI HOUSE

129-135 EAST DE VARGAS STREET (PRIVATE RESIDENCE)

ALTHOUGH ITS exact building date is unknown, this house in the BARRIO DE ANALCO was in existence in 1841 when it was owned by Italian-born trader Roque Tudesqui. Many of its adobe walls are more than 3 feet thick.

Roque Tudesqui was a successful businessman who acquired much property in Santa Fe. The census of 1839 listed him as "38 years old, single, trader." The fact that he was Italian by birth, an uncommon nationality for New Mexico traders, is revealed in the record of his marriage, in 1842, to María Ignacia Larrañaga.

Among the later owners of the property were the firm of Ardinger and Rumley; Reuben Frank Green, who in 1846 had operated the famous Exchange Hotel at the present site of La Fonda; and William L. Jones, who sold the western portion to Bertha L. Cartwright in 1895, thus dividing the house into two sections as it presently exists. In his will, probated in 1899, Mr. Jones left the eastern portion of the house in trust to the Episcopal Church of the Holy Faith. The church sold the property in 1921.

In late spring a beautiful wisteria blooms in the patio of the eastern portion of the house. The wisteria is at least 75 years old, and its trailing vines, now grown over an old tree, enhance the ancient street.

13
GREGORIO CRESPIN HOUSE

132 EAST DE VARGAS STREET (PRIVATE RESIDENCE)

AT THE WESTERN END of the BARRIO DE ANALCO, this house was part of the property owned in 1747 by Gregorio Crespin, who sold it for 50 *pesos* to Bartolomé Marquez with its "lands and an apricot tree." Tree-ring specimens taken from *vigas* in the house indicate their cutting date as 1720-50, and thick adobe walls testify further to its antiquity. The Territorial trim was added in the 19th century.

The property was owned between 1850 and 1862 by Don Blas Roibal, whose son, Benito, sold it in 1867 to Don Anastacio Sandoval, for whom Sandoval Street was named. The house was described as containing five rooms, a *portal* and a *placita*, with "free entry and exit on the north side." For many years it was known locally as the Van Stone House.

The land itself was part of a tract granted by General de Vargas to Juan de León Brito, a Tlaxcalan Indian who participated in the reconquest of 1693. This grant was later validated by Governor Domingo de Bustamante in 1738.

In the "Affidavit of Expenses" for the rebuilding of SAN MIGUEL CHAPEL in 1710, Juan and his brother, Diego Brito, are credited with a contribution, "as alms," of 1,500 adobe bricks for its construction, out of the 21,000 that were used to complete the building.

14
CHAPEL OF SAN MIGUEL

THE ORIGINAL CHAPEL of San Miguel had already been built in 1626 for the use of Indians from the BARRIO DE ANALCO when Custodian Fray Alonso de Benavides came to Santa Fe. No portion of this building is now visible. The Pueblo Revolt of 1680 began with the burning of San Miguel chapel. When de Vargas returned in 1693, he wrote that the walls were standing but repairs were not made, and in 1710 the chapel was completely rebuilt. Archeo-

logical excavations in 1955 revealed the details of the rebuilding. The original sanctuary, which was square instead of angled, was uncovered together with its adobe altars and steps. The 1710 outer walls had been placed on separate foundations beside the older ones. The main beam of the choir loft is inscribed: "The Lord Marquess de la Peñuela had this built by his aide, Royal Ensign Don Agustín Flores de Vergara in the year 1710." The date was confirmed by tree-ring cores taken from that and other beams, corbels and moldings in the chapel.

The expenses of rebuilding were borne by the military confraternity of San Miguel, to whose use the chapel was dedicated until the newer military chapel of LA CASTRENSE was erected on the Plaza in 1760. The interior contains many good examples of 18th century religious art in addition to its fine architectural woodwork. The gilded statue of St. Michael, the patron, is representative of *estofado* sculpture at its peak in old Mexico. The statue was already in Santa Fe in 1709 when it was taken in procession over the entire colony to raise money, goods, or services for the rebuilding of the chapel.

Seven of the oil paintings on canvas were sent from Mexico about the middle of the 18th century. Before this time, the adobe sanctuary walls were painted with marbleized columns and flowering urns. The largest painting of St. Michael was the work of Captain Bernardo Miera y Pacheco, more famous for the maps of the Southwest which he made in the 1770's. He came to Santa Fe in 1756, and presumably did the painting before 1760, when the new military chapel became the fashionable one. Although Miera did not sign his work, it is inscribed with the name of the donor, Manuel Sanz de Garvizu, lieutenant of the Santa Fe presidio and owner of the ARIAS DE QUIROS property at the time.

The painted altar screen with its spiral pillars was made in 1798, as may be seen in the two inscriptions at the bottom which state that the screen was made and painted that year at the expense of Antonio José Ortiz. Ortiz, possibly the richest man in New Mexico at the time, was the most generous contributor to the construction of church buildings. The retablo was designed to set off the eight paintings on canvas, and therefore had no images of holy persons painted on it as did many altar screens in rural churches.

The bell, which formerly hung in the tower and is now to be seen in the gift shop of the chapel, was cast in Santa Fe by an itinerant bell-caster, Francisco Luján, in 1856. Defects in the sand-casting made the date appear to be 1356, which has led to some confusion about the age of the bell. However, eyewitnesses of the casting of the bell, and its later installation in San Miguel tower, were still alive in 1914 and left exact accounts of the making.

San Miguel's appearance has changed many times. The 1710 church had a small belfry and adobe battlements on the roof like a fortress church of 16th century Mexico. In the early 19th century, it had a triple-tiered tower which collapsed in the 1870's, to be rebuilt in 1887 with a square tower and shuttered louvers, since removed. San Miguel served as a parish church for the south side of the river, but it has been neglected for long periods. In 1859, Bishop Lamy brought the Christian Brothers to Santa Fe to operate a school for boys. They bought the property and chapel, managing a school and college until recently, when the school and college were moved and the property, except for the chapel, was acquired by the State of New Mexico for additional capital buildings.

15 ST. MICHAEL'S DORMITORY

ERECTED IN 1878 by the Brothers of the Christian Schools, this building was for many years the main structure of St. Michael's College. It was originally three stories high and was the highest and largest adobe building in Santa Fe. Typical late 19th century details included a tower, porticos, galleries and a mansard roof. Administration, class and faculty rooms occupied the first two floors, while the third floor was used as a dormitory.

The Christian Brothers were brought to Santa Fe by Bishop Lamy in 1859 to establish a school for boys. For nearly 20 years, St. Michael's was housed in a much-remodeled single-story building. Funds to construct the new facility were raised by Brother Botulph, veteran educator and first director of the college, who went through the territory in 1877 seeking contributions. In addition to money and building materials, the record of donations listed

735 sheep, 2 young oxen, a heifer worth $8 and 2 goats valued at $1 each.

A disastrous fire in 1926 destroyed the tower and the third floor, which were not rebuilt. The appearance of the building was thus greatly altered, but the graceful two-story rear *portal* is one of the few remaining in Santa Fe. The French-style trim around the doors and windows and the original mansard roof were due to the influence of Archbishop Lamy and the early Christian Brothers, all of whom were native Frenchmen.

After 1947, when St. Michael's College (now named The College of Santa Fe) was organized as a separate unit and moved to the southern part of town, this building served as the dormitory for St. Michael's High School. The property was sold to the State of New Mexico in 1965 and now houses state offices. It has been renamed the Lamy Building.

16 THE "OLDEST HOUSE"

215 EAST DE VARGAS STREET

THE ORIGINS OF THIS house seem to be lost, but for almost a century tradition has called it the oldest house in Santa Fe. It was labeled the "oldest building" in the city on the Stoner map of 1882, and the Urrutia map of 1766-68 shows a structure near the CHAPEL OF SAN MIGUEL in the approximate position of this house. Tree-ring specimens, taken from some of the *vigas* in the ceilings of the lower rooms, show cutting dates of 1740-67.

On July 31, 1881, the house, although not specifically mentioned in deeds of title, was sold for $3,000 by Archbishop Lamy to the Brothers of the Christian Schools, popularly known as the Christian Brothers, with the CHAPEL OF SAN MIGUEL and other property. For decades this house was included in descriptions pertaining to the area immediately surrounding the CHAPEL OF SAN MIGUEL.

The house had two stories in 19th century photographs and paintings. In 1902, when the building was badly in need of repair, the second story was removed. The house remained a one-story structure until about a quarter of a century later, when a new second story was added. Presently, the eastern portion is rented as a curio shop, while the western part remains a unique remnant of the type of building once prevalent in the city—part Indian, part Spanish, low-ceilinged and crude, with dirt floors and thick adobe walls.

17
BOYLE HOUSE

327 EAST DE VARGAS STREET (PRIVATE RESIDENCE)

THIS LARGE ADOBE house east of the BARRIO DE ANALCO has had a long history. It appears on the Urrutia map of 1766-68 as a sizable, hacienda-type building, and also shows on the Gilmer map of 1846. Who the earliest owners were is unknown, but in the early 1800's, the house and outlying lands constituted the *rancho* of Salvador Martín, who conveyed the property to Antonio de Jesús Ortiz, son of the famous, wealthy landowner, Antonio José Ortiz. In his will of 1837, Antonio de Jesús bequeathed the property to his daughter Ana María, wife of Juan José Romero. She sold it to the Very Reverend Peter Eguillon, vicar general to Bishop Lamy, in 1863, and 4 years later the church conveyed it to Morris Bloomfield and Colonel Herbert M. Enos of the quartermaster corps.

Bloomfield sold his interest to telegraph operator Joseph Gough and his wife in 1874, and Enos and the new owners divided the property along the line of a hall which ran through the house. Shortly thereafter, Enos left New Mexico after providing that his half, on the east, be held in trust for his two minor and illegitimate daughters. The trustee was James L. Johnson, then owner of EL ZAGUAN. In 1881, the Goughs sold the west portion to Arthur Boyle, son-in-law of and New Mexico representative for English land speculator William Blackmore and his wife Blanche. The property was again joined in 1889 when the Enos daughters conveyed the east section to Blanche Blackmore Boyle. The Boyles added a northern tier of rooms to what remained of the original structure, and members of the family still own the house.

Massive adobe walls, in some places more than 4 feet thick, and ceilings of *rajas,* or split wood, overlaid with straw and earth, are evidence that the house was built at an early date. Territorial details include typical squared-off ceiling beams, a long rear *portal,* a manteled fireplace, and a bay window at the back of the house.

18 ADOLPH BANDELIER HOUSE

352 EAST DE VARGAS STREET (PRIVATE RESIDENCE)

THE MOST famous occupant of this large adobe house was Adolph Francis Bandelier, pioneer archeologist and ethnohistorian who made it his home while conducting research in New Mexico, Arizona, and Mexico during the years 1882-92.

The building is Territorial in style and has been extensively enlarged and remodeled without, however, losing its integrity. The first deed of record is the sale of the property to Marta Romero y Maynas, February 1, 1867, in which the house was described as having "three and one-half portals," of which only the one on the west still remains. The front entrance then faced south. In 1873, it was bought by John F. Schuman, who rented it to Bandelier.

Born in Berne, Switzerland, in 1840, Bandelier made his first trip to New Mexico in 1880. After a year of archeological investigation in Mexico and Central America, he returned to Santa Fe and spent much of the next 10 years conducting his research in the region. He was the first scholar to at-

tempt a comprehensive, scientific study of the archeology, ethnography, and historical documentation of the New Mexico Indians. He traveled thousands of miles on foot and horseback and often lived for weeks at a time in Indian villages.

He was author of *The Delight Makers,* a novel of prehistoric Pueblo Indians, major scientific works and articles on anthropological and historical subjects.

On February 11, 1914, shortly before Bandelier's death in Seville, Spain, President Woodrow Wilson proclaimed the ruins of Indian cliff dwellers in Frijoles Canyon the Bandelier National Monument.

In December, 1919, the house was bought by Santa Fe merchant Henry S. Kaune, whose wife was Elise C. Bandelier, a niece of the famous anthropologist. The new owners made extensive additions to the house. The property is still owned by the Kaune family.

19 ACEQUIA MADRE

THE OLD *acequias,* or irrigation ditches, of Santa Fe are almost things of the past, but the Acequia Madre—"Mother Ditch"—still flows along the street which bears its name and reminds us of what was once a vital part of the city's existence.

In the southeast section of Santa Fe, this *acequia* is still important to many persons who use its water to irrigate their fruit trees and grazing lands.

Ditch irrigation had long been used in the arid regions of Spain, as well as by Indians of the Southwest, and when the Spanish colonists came they brought both the engineering knowledge and body of irrigation law necessary to build and regulate water systems throughout the province of New Mexico. For more than 300 years these *acequia* systems have operated effectively. In rural areas and many towns they are still maintained and cherished.

Shortly after the founding of Santa Fe, both the *acequia madre* on the south side of town and the *acequia de la muralla* skirting the low hills on the north were built to provide water for irrigation and the domestic needs of the community. In the Urrutia map of the 1760's, the line of the northern *acequia* may be traced along the early wall, or *muralla,* which helped fortify the city, at the approx-imate location of present Hillside Avenue. In the early Spanish period, water for the PALACE OF THE GOVERNORS came from two *acequias* which apparently ran from the *cienega,* or springs, to the east. One flowed down present Palace Avenue in front of the building; the other watered gardens in the rear. By cutting off the water from these *acequias,* the Indians forced the Spaniards to evacuate in the Pueblo Revolt and by the same method, de Vargas drove the Indians out of the Palace in 1693. Later, other *acequias* carried water to the ecclesiastical lands and adjoining property in the city.

No recognizable traces of these *acequias* remain, but the Acequia Madre has never ceased to flow, and it is still governed by the old Spanish laws, with a *mayordomo de la acequia* and three commissioners to supervise its upkeep. An annual fee is paid by all property owners along the ditch who still hold water rights, and it is their duty to help clean out the *acequia* in the spring, as well as to assist when further help is needed during the irrigation season.

20 CANYON ROAD

CANYON ROAD IS THE center of Santa Fe's art colony and one of the older districts of the city. Before the Spanish conquest, an Indian trail along the Santa Fe River followed the course of the present street and led over the Sangre de Cristo Mountains to the pueblo of Pecos. Spanish authorities designated the trail as *el camino del cañon* ("the road of the canyon"). After crossing the mountains, it joined the main road to Pecos on the plain east of town.

Until quite recently, the road was used by woodcutters to bring firewood, heavily loaded on the backs of their burros, to customers in the city.

For many years, lower Canyon Road was the scene of the annual Corpus Christi procession, which was routed from St. Francis Cathedral along the Alameda to the old Castillo Street Bridge (since replaced by a wider structure), then up to Canyon Road under flower-trimmed arches to the Delgado Street corner. Here, the archbishop pronounced benediction before an altar erected for the occasion by the Delgado family.

Beginning at the corner of García Street and extending far up the canyon, the winding, narrow street has succeeded in retaining much of its character, in part because of the number of old adobe structures along its informal street line. Many of these houses are built almost flush with the pavement. They contain shops, art galleries, studios, restaurants, and neighborhood services appropriate to Canyon Road's designation by city ordinance as a "residential arts and crafts zone." The unpaved streets that branch off Canyon Road and Acequia Madre, irregular, shady, and narrow, look very much as they did in the past.

The old Indian trail over the mountain was reopened in 1900 by rangers from the Pecos River Forest Reserve. In 1932, however, the Public Service Company closed the Santa Fe Canyon to visitors. The road is populated for approximately 4 miles.

21 JUAN JOSE PRADA HOUSE

519 CANYON ROAD (PRIVATE RESIDENCE)

ACCORDING TO EARLY maps, this house may have been in existence as early as 1768, although its first date of record is over 100 years later. In 1869, when it was owned by Juan José Prada, it consisted of two sections, with a corridor running from north to south between them. At that time he deeded the west section to Altagracia Arrañaga, and in 1882 his widow deeded the east section to her son-in-law, Miguel Gorman, a descendant of one of the soldiers in the U.S. Army of Occupation. The deeds stipulated that the front door of the corridor be left open to allow access to a *baile* (dance) hall in the rear, and that the well in front of the house, which is still standing, was to be free for the use of those living in both sections. During the late 19th century the brick *pretil*, or coping, was added to the roof by artisans who built ST. FRANCIS CATHEDRAL.

In 1927 the east wing was purchased as a residence by the late Mrs. Charles S. Dietrich, who added other rooms and modernized its interior without changing its classic Territorial style of architecture. Later she acquired the west section of the house and joined the two together, but without the original connecting corridor.

Still intact at the northern end of the property is a small barn of *jacal* construction—squared-off cedar logs more than 30 inches in circumference, set upright in the ground with cracks chinked of adobe (picture on page 7). This type of construction was often used in New Mexico.

The first owner of record, Juan José Prada, was a descendant of José Prada, a native of Chihuahua, who came to Santa Fe as a soldier in the Santa Fe garrison of the Spanish army.

22
EL ZAGUAN

ONE OF THE ARCHITECTURAL treasures of New Mexico, this rambling old hacienda and its garden stretch more than 300 feet along lower CANYON ROAD. Named El Zaguán because of its long covered corridor, running from the large garden at the west to an open patio at the east, the building now contains 19 rooms which have been converted into private rental apartments of various sizes.

When it was bought in 1849 by James L. Johnson, a prominent merchant during the days of the Santa Fe Trail, it was of Spanish Pueblo style and consisted of two or three rooms, which can be identified by their 4-foot-thick adobe walls. Mr. Johnson came to New Mexico from Maryland at the age of

20, and later owned a general store on the northeast corner of the Plaza. He added more rooms to his residence, with walls 3 feet thick, including a "chocolate room" where chocolate was ground and served each afternoon, a "treasure room" with barred windows where the family valuables were kept, a private chapel, and a semidetached room overlooking the west garden for his library, said to have been the largest in the territory. Architecturally, these later rooms were Territorial in style, which accounts for the brick coping on the roof. At one time the house contained 24 rooms, with servants' quarters across the street.

On the lower terrace behind the houses were orchards, a cornfield, and large corrals where freigh-

40

ters on the Santa Fe Trail kept their horses and oxen before making the return trip.

The large west garden (picture on page 78) was laid out by Adolph Bandelier, and its peony bushes, imported from China more than 100 years ago, are still flourishing. The two large horse chestnut trees, which were planted by Johnson, have become city landmarks.

As the home of Colonel and Mrs. James Baca, Johnson's grandson, the property was long known as the Baca Place, but in 1927 it passed out of the family. Threatened with demolition to make way for a modern apartment building, it was bought by Mrs. Charles H. Dietrich. A private girls' school known as Brownmoor was housed in the building during the early 1930's. Later, the house was converted into rental apartments without changing its exterior appearance. Even the old well still remains under the back *portal*.

After the owner's death in 1961, the building was again bought for preservation, this time by El Zaguan, Inc., and one of its apartments is now used as an office by the Old Santa Fe Association.

In 1960 the building was measured and recorded by the Historical American Buildings Survey for the Library of Congress in Washington.

41

23
OLIVE RUSH STUDIO

ONE OF THE FEW ADOBE houses remaining in Santa Fe that has not been covered with concrete stucco for preservation, the Olive Rush Studio is typical of those purchased by artists and writers who flocked to Santa Fe and Taos during the first two decades of this century. Drawn primarily by their wish to record on canvas or in words the life of the Indian and the beauty of the landscape, they found in New Mexico a place which the artist Frederic Remington described in 1902 as having been overlooked by the "heavy-handed God of Progress."

When Olive Rush, internationally known Quaker artist, first came to Santa Fe in 1914, she was so impressed by the country that she returned 6 years later to make it her permanent home. At that time she bought this house, which had been in the Sena and Rodríguez families for several generations, and it has been kept in very much its original state ever since. Its thick adobe walls, deep side *portal,* and charming back garden are all typical of the period, although efforts to document the exact building date have been unsuccessful. In the early days there were no surveys, deeds were usually not filed, and descriptions of property were often confusing and inaccurate, particularly in the CANYON ROAD area where landowners knew their own boundaries and respected those of their neighbors.

During the past several years this building has served as a meeting house for the Santa Fe Religious Society of Friends, of which the late Miss Rush was a birthright member.

24
BORREGO HOUSE

724 CANYON ROAD

EARLY RECORDS FOR many houses in this area have not been found. There is, however, a Spanish deed for the property in which the Borrego House is located dated September 14, 1753, at which time it was sold to Gerónimo López by Ysidro Martín, a soldier in the Spanish Army, who may originally have received it as a grant for military service. The conveyance was for farm land described as bounded on the south by the Acequia Madre and on the north by "a Royal Road which comes down from the mountain range," now known as Canyon Road.

In his will dated 1769, Gerónimo López stated that he owned two houses, one newly built, adjoining an orchard of 14 trees and farm land. His widow later sold the property to Gerónimo Gonzáles, and because she was unable to write her name, Gonzáles, as buyer, witnessed the deed for her. In 1839, he in turn sold it to his son-in-law, Rafael Borrego, and for more than 75 years thereafter it was owned by members of the Borrego family.

During the late 19th century, the Borregos added the large front room, and as they were prominent in New Mexico political circles, it was probably the scene of many political gatherings and social events. The long front *portal* with tapered, hand-hewn columns, windows, and doors, typical of the territorial period, may have been added at the same time.

When Rafael Borrego died, sometime between 1839 and 1845, half of the property was inherited by his children and the other half by his widow, María Refugio Gonzáles de Borrego. When she died in 1872, she left her residence—a three-room house with a hall and *portal*—to her son, Pablo. A room *abajo* ("below") was willed to a servant. It was a common practice in those days to bequeath individual rooms, and sometimes parts of rooms, to one's children as their inheritance, thereby creating many deed complications for later generations to untangle. It was not until 1939 that all portions of the house came again into a single ownership.

By 1906, the property had passed out of Borrego hands, and after a series of different owners the main portion of the house was bought for preservation in 1928 by Mrs. Charles H. Dietrich, who had acquired El Zaguan for the same purpose the previous year. In 1939, she bought the remaining two rooms and had the house restored under the supervision of Mrs. Kenneth L. Chapman. In 1931, the house received the Cyrus McCormick prize for the best restoration of a residence during the preceding 2 years. In 1940, the house was selected for study by the Historic American Buildings Survey, and drawings of its plans are now on file in the Library of Congress.

After later ownerships, when the future of the famous old house seemed endangered, it was bought by the Old Santa Fe Association for preservation and is rented as a coffee house and restaurant.

25
DE LA PEÑA HOUSE

831 EL CAMINITO (PRIVATE RESIDENCE)

NOTED FOR ITS EARLY 19th century Spanish Pueblo architecture on both the exterior and interior, this house was occupied for almost 80 years by the de la Peña family, for whom Calle Peña was named. The Historic American Building Survey of 1941, edited by the National Park Service, lists the house as one of the eight Santa Fe buildings of historical importance to the United States, and photographs of it taken in 1937 are in the Library of Congress.

The earliest date of record for the property is May 3, 1845, when it was sold by Tomás de Jesús López to Sergeant Francisco de la Peña for $114. It was described as a piece of farm land with a "house of four rooms and a *portal* situated in said land." The original east *portal,* which contains a shepherd's bed, is now an enclosed room. The property transfer of 1845 and subsequently involved "agricultural land" and referred to numerous *acequias* on or bordering the property. None of these runs today.

Sergeant de la Peña was a regular army soldier who served in the presidial companies of both Santa Fe and San Miguel before being mustered out June 18, 1846. He was with the military force which negotiated a peace treaty with the Navajo in 1835, and participated in two campaigns against the Indians, as well as one against the Texas Expedition of 1841 for which he received the Shield of Honor award.

When Francisco de la Peña died in 1887, he left his wife, Isabelita Rodríguez de la Peña, and eight children. After her death, the property was divided in 1909 among the six surviving children, each receiving a portion of the land, six *vigas* of the house, and free entrance and exit to it. Two daughters were still living there in 1925.

In 1925 and 1926 Frank G. Applegate purchased the house and land from the surviving Peña heirs. He enlarged the house, built the second story, and had the beam, which was on the front *portal,* raised to that level and a copy of it installed on the first-floor *portal.* Authentic details incorporated into the house at that time were Spanish Colonial balconies, taken from an old building, three old New Mexican *trasteros* built into the walls, squared beams, and corbels. Some of the walls are 3 feet thick in the four original rooms, two of which are combined in the present living room.

Mr. Applegate, who died in 1931, was a well-known writer and artist and one of the first leaders in Santa Fe to take a major interest in local crafts. He and the writer Mary Austin were active in organizing a group which provided funds for the repair of the church at las Trampas and the mission churches of Ácoma, Laguna and Zia. The group also purchased the Santuario de Chimayó, which was then a private chapel, restored it, and gave it to the Catholic Church.

26
CHURCH OF CRISTO REY

ALTHOUGH OF RECENT construction, the parish Church of Cristo Rey is a classic example of New Mexico mission architecture of the Spanish period. It was designed primarily as a fitting sanctuary for the great stone *reredos,* or altar screen,

48

which had originally been in LA CASTRENSE on the Plaza, the most famous Spanish colonial work of ecclesiastical art created in New Mexico and the prototype for the many hand-hewn wooden altar screens of the early period. The church was built in commemoration of the 400th anniversary of Coronado's exploration of the Southwest.

One of the largest modern adobe structures in existence, the church was designed by Santa Fe architect John Gaw Meem and built by contractor Fred Grill in the spirit and tradition of the old Spanish missions, with parishioners doing much of the labor under professional supervision. The 180,000 adobe bricks which went into its construction were made in the traditional way from the soil on which the church stands, and much of the woodwork, including the hard-carved corbels, was done at the site from the architect's design.

The building was dedicated on June 27, 1940, by Archbishop Rudolphus Aloysius Gerken, who had made the first two adobe bricks for its construction. One of these disappeared the night of the dedication, but the other is still lodged in the south tower.

The beautiful hand-carved *reredos* behind the altar was originally commissioned in 1760 by Governor Francisco Antonio Marín del Valle for the military chapel. Made of native white stone from a quarry near Jacona, it was carved and painted by Mexican artisans brought to Santa Fe by Governor Marín del Valle. The work was done within the old chapel on the Plaza, as evidenced by chippings and small carved pieces of stone like that of the *reredos* which were found on the site when LA CASTRENSE was excavated in 1955.

The carved stone plaque of Our Lady of Light in half-relief which is embedded in the central panel was originally installed in the wall above the entrance to LA CASTRENSE. At the top of the *reredos* is the figure of God, and beneath Him a panel of Our Lady of Valvanera. Below this St. James the Apostle is depicted on horseback, with St. Joseph on his right and St. John Nepomuk on his left. The lower left panel contains St. Ignatius Loyola, and the lower right St. Francis of Solano. The intricate design is similar to that found in 16th century European and 17th century Mexican churches, from which it was derived.

27
RANDALL DAVEY HOUSE

UPPER CANYON ROAD (MAY BE SEEN BY APPOINTMENT)

THE PROPERTY WAS part of the Ta- laya Hill grant given in 1731 to Manuel Trujillo. Far from the plaza in Spanish days, it was used only for grazing and woodcutting until the first sawmill in Santa Fe was built there by the U.S. Army quarter- master in 1847 to provide lumber for FORT MARCY, then under construction. The main house still shows the stone walls and huge, hand-hewn timbers of the mill on the interior, carefully preserved by the late

owner, Randall Davey, an artist of international reputation.

In 1852, the property was sold at public auction and was described as including one mile of river frontage, "one grist mill, one circular sawmill with extra gearing; the building for said sawmill is a good two story building, built for that purpose. Also two dwelling houses and one stable." The highest bidder at $500 was Colonel Ceran St. Vrain, a well-known trader and trapper from St. Louis. After some litigation over mortgages to St. Vrain by temporary operators of the mill, St. Vrain sold the mill machinery to Joseph Hirsch and Isaiah Smith in 1856 to be moved to another site. In 1864, the mill and land had come into possession of Louis Gold, another local trader, who bought it from Benito Borrego and his wife, María del Carmen Martínez, and José Candelario Martínez. The Martínezes were descendants of Nicolás Ortiz III, a powerful figure of 18th century Santa Fe.

By 1892, the present Davey property was owned by Captain Candelario Martínez, a native of Santa Fe who enlisted in the First Infantry, New Mexico Volunteers, at the age of 18. He was promoted to captain when he recaptured United States mail

from Kiowa and Comanche Indians on the plains and survived a gunshot wound in the melee. Martínez later became an attorney and held positions as postmaster and probate judge in Santa Fe. In 1906, a United States patent signed by President Theodore Roosevelt was issued for the property.

Randall Davey bought the stone mill and other buildings in 1920, and made it his home and studio for over 40 years. He furnished the home in tasteful style, combining New Mexican and European pieces. The Davey studio remains as it was during the years that he painted in it, while the former stables are a gallery where a series of the artist's works in his varied styles is exhibited. The remaining old building is now a guesthouse.

28 JUAN RODRIGUEZ HOUSE

CERRO GORDO & GONZALES ROADS (PRIVATE RESIDENCE)

VERY LITTLE OF THIS house can be seen today, but the older part is of architectural interest because of its 19th century New Mexican detail. Built around two patios, the house was Spanish Pueblo, and when it was sold by the Rodríguez family in 1923 to Mr. and Mrs. S. C. Hamilton, modernization was done with little alteration. There was a one-room house in 1844. As early as 1756 the first gristmill in Santa Fe was built by Vicar Santiago Roybal on the land in the riverbed, now a city park at the east end of the Alameda. The mill, called El Molino de San Francisco, was noted by Fray Francisco Atanasio Domínguez in 1776 as one of three then in Santa Fe.

In 1868, it was referred to as El Molino de las Animas by the owner, Juan Rodríguez y Ortiz, who left it to his wife, María Juana Quintana, with a house of five rooms. While the Rodríguez family owned the property it extended west of Palace Avenue, north to the top of the hills, south to CANYON ROAD and east to the Public Service Company's powerhouse opposite the CHURCH OF CRISTO REY. In the 1880's, the city acquired a right of way to extend Gonzales Road to the Santa Fe River.

Vicar Roybal's mill was in use until 1911, when the Public Service Company cut off the water supply from the river. Until the 1920's, ruins of the old mill could be seen. Old-timers recall that Teodoro Martínez, the miller, collected 2½ *fanegas* of flour for grinding a wagonload of grain.

Most of the present structures on the Juan Rodríguez property were remodeled or built in 1969-70.

29 FRANCISCA HINOJOS HOUSE

355 EAST PALACE AVENUE (PRIVATE RESIDENCE)

DESIGNED AND constructed by itinerant French artisans who were brought here from Louisiana by Archbishop Lamy to build ST. FRANCIS CATHEDRAL, this late 19th century residence is of special interest because of its unusual architectural detail. Although built of adobe, its exterior design and roof are more typical of Louisiana's architecture during French occupation than of Santa Fe's.

The trim of the interior doors, windows, and Territorial fireplaces is also of interest, for it typifies the period when craftsmen excelled in imitating such grained woods as mahogany, oak, and bird's-eye maple, in this case on woodwork of native pine. The retaining wall in front of the house is of stone left over from the building of the Cathedral, and is similar in architectural treatment.

The land on which the house was built was part of a property that once included Martinez Street, the site of the present hotel La Posada, and East Palace Avenue itself, which before 1870 extended only to the eastern end of SENA PLAZA. Beyond that were open fields and a path leading along the irrigation ditch known as Acequia de la Loma.

A member of a distinguished Santa Fe family which originally arrived here from Mexico in the early 1700's, Doña Francisca Hinojos acquired the property at intervals between 1856 and 1870. In 1887 she bequeathed it to her son, Don Alfredo Hinojos, a prominent political figure, who was organist at the Cathedral for almost 50 years.

The small rear building with a hutch roof was formerly the kitchen for the main house.

30 SENA PLAZA

THE LAND ON WHICH Sena Plaza now stands was once part of the property granted to Captain Arias de Quiros by General Diego de Vargas, with whom he campaigned during the reconquest of New Mexico in 1693. By the will of Juan Nepomuceno Alaríd, dated 1844, this portion of the ARIAS DE QUIROS property passed to his sister, María del Rosario Alaríd, wife of Juan Estevan Sena, and thence to their son, José D. Sena, who was a major in the United States army during the Civil War.

At the time of Don José's marriage in 1864 to Doña Isabel Cabeza de Baca, daughter of an equally prominent Santa Fe family, the property included a *placita* to the west and a small adobe house, which eventually increased to become an hacienda containing 33 rooms. All of these were on the first floor except for the second-story ballroom added to the west side. This was reached, as it is today, by an outside stairway. After the territorial capitol burned on May 13, 1892, this ballroom served as a meeting place for the legislative assembly until it could be housed elsewhere.

The family of Don José, which included 11 children, lived on the south, east, and west sides of the

54

inner patio, where guests were always welcomed with Spanish hospitality. A coach house, storerooms, a chicken house and servants' quarters occupied space on the north. The well at the east and two front entrances remain in their original location, but a well at the west has been filled in.

Upon the death of Major Sena and his wife the land was divided into equal strips, 16½ *varas* in width, for the six surviving children. In 1927 these heirs deeded the property to the late Senator Bronson M. Cutting, the late Miss Martha R. White, and Miss Amelia E. White, who restored and remodeled the building for preservation. The original two-story portion at the west had been deeded to Dr. Frank E. Mera, who added it to the restoration project. The heirs reserved the right, however, to erect the family altar under the *portal* facing Palace Avenue for the annual Corpus Christi procession,

and for many years thereafter it was a colorful part of this religious celebration.

The second story on the eastern and northern portions of the building was added in 1927, when the property changed hands. This work was done under the supervision of the late William Penhallow Henderson, a well-known Santa Fe artist, designer and builder, and it is a classic example of how a historic building can be restored and reconstructed to adapt to modern business requirements, and yet keep the integrity of the original.

Because of the long, continuous *portal* in front of the Sena, Prince, and Trujillo buildings on this site, the inclusive name "Sena Plaza" is often given locally to the entire building complex. The above data refer only to the building and patio at its eastern end and not to those on the west.

31
ARIAS DE QUIROS SITE

EAST PALACE AVENUE

DIEGO ARIAS DE QUIROS, a native of Asturias, Spain, received this land from General de Vargas as a reward for his services in the reconquest of New Mexico in 1693. Arias was a member of the Cofradía de la Conquistadora and of the military Cofradía de San Miguel in Santa Fe. The land adjoined the eastern *torreón* of the PALACE OF THE GOVERNORS, ran east to the *cienega,* including the location of the present Coronado Medical Building, and north to Nusbaum Street. It was sufficiently large to plant 2½ *fanegas* of wheat. Arias de Quiros died in 1738 and the property, which included a two-room house with a *zaguán,* was sold by his wid-

ow in 1746 to Manuel Sáenz de Garvizu, lieutenant of the Santa Fe presidio, for 300 *pesos* of silver marked by the mint of Mexico City. The original house on the property probably vanished long ago, and the land has been subdivided and built over, but one of the structures may date back to the 18th century.

In 1879, L. Bradford Prince, newly appointed territorial supreme court justice for New Mexico, purchased the western portion from Carmen Benavides de Roubidoux of Costilla County, Colorado. The house was described as "consisting of seven rooms and according to the old description, sixty-

one vigas." Carmen was the widow of Antoine Roubidoux, famous French-Canadian trader and interpreter for General Kearny in 1846. Antoine first came to Santa Fe about 1823, became a naturalized citizen in 1829, and the next year was elected to the Ayuntamiento (town council). As he married Carmen Benavides in 1828, their occupancy of the house may have begun at that time. They no longer made New Mexico their home after the middle 1830's, and the residents of the house until the purchase by Prince are unknown.

The 109 East Palace structure, sometimes known as the Trujillo Plaza, will be remembered historically as the first office of the Manhattan Project, now the U.S. Atomic Energy Commission, from 1943 to 1963.

The eastern section (111-119 East Palace) was the inheritance of Manuel G. Sena from his parents, Juan Estevan Sena and María del Rosario Alaríd.

Manuel Sena and his wife Concepción García lost the land to the Spiegelberg family through foreclosure in 1878, and after a series of owners, this property was also conveyed to Mr. and Mrs. L. Bradford Prince in 1886.

After his term as chief justice, Prince was governor of New Mexico, 1889-93, president of the Historical Society of New Mexico, chancellor of the New Mexico Missionary District of the Episcopal Church for 40 years, and author of several historical works.

During the Princes' residence, this house was the scene of many celebrated social events.

The 115 East Palace building was used as an AWVS Service club for enlisted men during the Second World War. Today, the series of buildings contains a restaurant, offices, and shops but preserves many architectural details of the Spanish, Mexican Republican, and U.S. Territorial periods.

57

32
CATHEDRAL OF ST. FRANCIS

BISHOP JEAN BAPTISTE LAMY be-
gan construction of the stone Cathedral of St. Francis in 1869 on the approximate site of earlier
churches. Designed in the Romanesque style of
Lamy's native Auvergne, the main building is architecturally foreign to Santa Fe's Spanish heritage and
Indian background, except for the adobe chapel of
Our Lady of the Rosary on the northeast which has
survived from the earlier *parroquia* (parish church).

58

The first church near the site, with an adjoining
convento, was built by Fray Alonso de Benavides
about 1628, but was destroyed in the Pueblo Revolt
of 1680. Its plan and exact location are unknown,
but it probably stood immediately behind the present Cathedral, facing to the west.

The adobe *parroquia* which preceded the present
Cathedral was built between 1714 and 1721. The
chapel of Our Lady of the Rosary formed the

northern portion of the transept and was dedicated to the small, 16th century wooden statue of the Virgin known affectionately since the early Spanish period as "La Conquistadora" (Our Lady of the Conquest). Brought to Santa Fe by Benavides about 1625, the statue was originally known as Our Lady of the Assumption. It was taken to the El Paso region by the retreating Spaniards in 1680, and accompanied General Diego de Vargas back to Santa Fe during the reconquest of 1693 when, according to legend, its intervention in behalf of the Spaniards saved them from harm.

The *parroquia* was in ruinous condition by 1798 when it was restored, including La Conquistadora chapel, largely at the expense of Antonio José Ortiz, the wealthy Santa Fe citizen who was also responsible for major repairs to the CHAPEL OF SAN MIGUEL. Ortiz also subsidized the construction of a second chapel, dedicated to San José, on the south side of the *parroquia*. This chapel was demolished during recent remodeling.

The stone for the 1869 Cathedral came from local quarries at the Arroyo Sais, Lamy Junction and the top of La Bajada Mesa. Much wider and half again as long as those of its predecessor, the walls of the new structure were built enclosing those of the *parroquia,* which remained in use until the nave was completed. The old adobe walls were then demolished and the rubble carted off. The choir loft and part of the walls of the chapel of Our Lady of the Rosary were removed, making the chapel shorter than it had been originally.

The Cathedral was never completed according to the original French plans, which called for steeples rising to a height of 160 feet on each of its two towers. Supervised first by an American architect who proved unequal to the task, the work was continued by a French father-and-son team named Mouly. Italian stone cutters were also employed, descendants of some of whom are still living in Santa Fe.

La Conquistadora chapel, in continuous use since 1718 although reduced in size, is still in many ways the most interesting portion of the Cathedral of St. Francis. It contains the only stone sarcophagus of the Spanish period, in which repose the bones of two 17th century friars who served at Picurís

and Quarai and were especially revered by their Indian converts. Their remains were brought to Santa Fe in 1759 by Governor Marín del Valle for reburial. The existing altar is composed of two side altars made in Mexico in 1748 and sent to Santa Fe as gifts. The chapel is also the permanent home of La Conquistadora, the little wooden statue which has been the symbol of special religious devotion and Hispanic unity from colonial times to the present.

33
LORETTO CHAPEL

THE WORLD-FAMOUS stone chapel of the Sisters of Loretto, known as "The Chapel of Our Lady of Light" was constructed as a part of the ambitious church building project of Archbishop Jean B. Lamy which culminated in the erecting of the present CATHEDRAL OF ST. FRANCIS. It was designed to serve the spiritual needs of the sisters and the students of the academy for girls which they had begun in January, 1853, shortly after six nuns of the

Order of Loretto had been brought to New Mexico by Lamy, then bishop.

Lamy turned over his own adobe two-story residence for the use of the sisters, and their first chapel was located there. From 1859 to 1863, the order acquired the large block of land on which their school, convent, and chapel were finally located. During the Confederate invasion of 1862, the nuns feared for the safety of their charges, and

Bishop Lamy appealed to the military commander and secured his protection of the institution from molestation.

Under the direction of the younger Mouly, masons began cutting the stone on January 19, 1874. After many interruptions, the delicately proportioned Gothic-style chapel with its rose window was blessed by Vicar-General Peter Eguillon on April 25, 1878. The 3-foot-high iron statue of Our Lady of Lourdes was placed on the pinnacle of the building 10 years later.

When the chapel was completed, there was no means of ascending to the choir loft, since the workmen felt that there was insufficient room to build a safe staircase. The sisters sought for someone who could devise a stairway. Shortly thereafter, a carpenter appeared and constructed the famous circular staircase, built without nails or other visible means of support. He then disappeared without waiting to be paid. Legend has persisted that it was the work of St. Joseph, the carpenter saint. One of the several European-born artisans living in Santa Fe at the time may have been the unknown carpenter, but recent information strongly suggests the possibility that the craftsman was Johann Hadwiger, an Austrian immigrant who had heard of the sisters' quest while visiting his son in a Colorado mining camp. The "miraculous" nature of the staircase is in no way dimmed by the probability of human construction.

The extensive property of the Sisters of Loretto was sold in 1971 for commercial development, but the chapel will continue to be maintained as a historical shrine.

34
PADRE GALLEGOS HOUSE

227-237 WASHINGTON AVENUE

SOON AFTER 1857, José Manuel Gallegos, a colorful and controversial priest who had been defrocked by Bishop Lamy 5 years earlier, built this house as his residence. Padre Gallegos was one of the most important figures in the stormy history of mid-19th-century New Mexico.

During and after the Civil War, part of the building was used as a rooming house. Included among its tenants was Major John Ayres, quartermaster at FORT MARCY, who lived in the house for 18 years. For a short period, the first Episcopal Church in Santa Fe, known as "The Good Shepherd Mission," was located in the north wing. As the mission was

established in 1868, the same year in which Padre Gallegos married Candelaria Montoya, a widow, it is probable that the wedding took place there. The marriage, performed by John Woart, who was chaplain of Fort Union, is the first entry in the parish register of the Episcopal Church of the Holy Faith in Santa Fe.

José Manuel Gallegos was born in Abiquiu, New Mexico, in 1815. His great-great grandfather, José Luis Valdéz, a native of Oviedo, Spain, had come to New Mexico as a colonist in 1693. After receiving his early education as a student of the rebellious Padre Martínez of Taos, José Manuel studied for

62

the priesthood in Durango, Mexico, where he was ordained in 1840. He ministered to various Indian pueblos and in Albuquerque, and also served in the departmental assembly of New Mexico from 1843 to 1846. Some historians believe he was one of the ringleaders in an attempted revolt against the Americans in December of 1846.

In 1851, while priest at San Felipe de Neri Church in Albuquerque, he was elected to the upper house of the first legislative assembly of the territory of New Mexico. His rebellion against church authorities began the same year with the arrival of Bishop Lamy. Having heard of Gallegos' gambling, dancing, and consorting with *politicos,* Lamy sent Vicar-General Machebeuf to Albuquerque to replace him. When Gallegos staged an open revolt, Bishop Lamy suspended him from ministering in the church. In a countermove, Padre Gallegos claimed he held deeds from the bishop of Durango to the priest's residence adjoining San Felipe de Neri Church. Although the documents were apparently forged, a suit instituted by Machebeuf was dismissed in 1856, probably by mutual consent.

In the interim, Padre Gallegos was elected to the position of territorial delegate to the U.S. Congress in 1853 and was reelected in 1855. He served in this session only until July of 1856, when he was unseated by Miguel A. Otero, who had contested the election. After moving to Santa Fe in 1857, Gallegos served four terms as speaker of the house in the legislative assembly and two years as territorial treasurer. In 1868, he was appointed superintendent of Indian Affairs by President Andrew Johnson.

One more term in the U.S. Congress during 1871 to 1873 ended the political career of Padre Gallegos. When death came from a stroke in 1875, the *Daily New Mexican* called him "the most universally known man in the Territory." His funeral, which was held at St. Francis Cathedral, was one of the largest ever witnessed in the city of Santa Fe. He was buried in Rosario Cemetery, where his marble tombstone still stands.

The Padre Gallegos house was remodeled and at the same time restored to its original proportions in 1966-67.

35
ROQUE LOBATO HOUSE

311 WASHINGTON AVENUE (PRIVATE RESIDENCE)

ONE OF THE oldest on record in Santa Fe, this house was built soon after 1785 by Roque Lobato, armorer and soldier of the Spanish royal garrison of Santa Fe, on land granted him by Governor Juan Bautista de Anza. In response to Lobato's petition for land which would enable him "to live, build a house, and cultivate land for the support of my family," the specific Act of Possession took place on September 26, 1785. As was the custom in making grants, an official formally took Lobato by the hand and put him in Royal Possession, while the witnesses present pulled up grass and threw stones and shouted "Long live the King, our Lord, may God bless him!"

Several entries in the Spanish archives reveal that Roque Lobato did not get along well with his neighbors. The most serious altercation occurred in 1765, when he was accused of assault and battery, and as punishment he and his wife, Josefa Armijo, were banished to Chimayó, New Mexico, for 3 years.

The next owner of the property was Jesús Ribera, also a soldier, who restored the house and lived in it for almost 50 years. It was probably during this period that a sentry house and watchtower, known as La Garita, was built northeast of the house, for there are no known records of this famous building until 1835, when Ribera leased it to the military authorities as a storehouse for gunpowder. In 1837 the leading insurrectionists of the "Chimayó Rebellion" were executed at La Garita for treason, after their uprising against Governor Albino Pérez had led to his assassination. After FORT MARCY was built, La Garita fell into disuse, and not even its ruins exist today.

In 1852, Ribera sold the house with its adjoining lands and La Garita to Don Gaspar Ortiz y Alaríd, a distinguished local citizen for whom Don Gaspar Avenue and Ortiz Street in Santa Fe were named. A second lieutenant in the Mexican army and close associate of General Manuel Armijo, the last governor to serve under Mexican rule, Ortiz y Alaríd fled with Armijo, other officers, and 40 dragoons to Mexico in 1846 to report the news of General Kearny's occupation of New Mexico. Captured and imprisoned by United States troops when he later reentered El Paso, he was paroled after a few days and returned to Santa Fe the following year.

Within a comparatively short time Don Gaspar established himself as a trader over the Santa Fe Trail and the Camino Real from Chihuahua, and erected a warehouse for his goods on the north side of San Francisco Street facing the street that bears his name. His adjoining real estate in the area extended as far south as the Santa Fe River. In 1848, he married Magdalena Lucero, and one of their daughters became the wife of Felipe B. Delgado, another Santa Fe trader.

At the outbreak of the Civil War, Ortiz y Alaríd was commissioned a captain in the Union army and took part in the battle of Glorieta Pass, 20 miles east of Santa Fe.

During the following years the property changed hands many times before it was bought in 1910 by Dr. Sylvanus G. Morley, a well-known archeologist who was a leader in the movement to revive the indigenous architecture of Santa Fe (Morley was director of the School of American Research and the Museum of New Mexico at the time of his death in 1948). He restored the old house with many interior changes and added a back *portal* in which he incorporated an elaborately carved beam and corbels, but retained the original Spanish Pueblo character of the architecture, including the front *portal*. The brick coping on the firewalls was added at a later date.

36
UNITED STATES COURT HOUSE

SOUTH FEDERAL PLACE

WHEN THIS LARGE building of native New Mexico stone was finally completed in 1889—36 years after construction began—it was considered one of the most handsome, up-to-date structures in the city. Today it stands as one of the very few remaining unaltered examples in the Southwest of the imposing public buildings of that period, once common particularly throughout the Midwest. Although the architectural style is Greek Revival and not indigenous to this area, its unusual history, good proportions, and honest materials make it worthy of inclusion among the historic buildings of Santa Fe.

The land on which it was built was part of the public grounds acquired by the United States from the Mexican government under the 1848 Treaty of Guadalupe Hidalgo. Immediately after the territory of New Mexico had been organized in 1850, the U.S. Congress appropriated an inadequate $20,000 for the construction of "a capitol building." In 1854, another $50,000 was added, but these funds were exhausted after only one and a half stories had been built above the basement, and for the next 25 years the building stood without a roof and in a state of "increasing dilapidation."

An 1860 appropriation of $60,000 to complete the building was never paid as a result of New Mexico's exemption from special war taxes during the Civil War.

Further attempts were made during the 1860's and 70's to finish construction, as it was necessary to rent other space for the functions of the federal courts and territorial legislature. Among the appeals sent to Washington was one explaining the lack of competent workmen to cut the stone for the building, which was "of the hardest nature and very difficult to cut," and another that "all the tools to work with must be brought from the States" as no such equipment was available in New Mexico. The rough stone for the walls was quarried in the Hyde Park region of Santa Fe, and the dressed stone in Cerrillos, New Mexico.

Except for these appeals, the half-built structure, which was said to bear a striking resemblance to "the hulk of a coal barge," was neglected until the summer of 1883, when the grounds around the building were selected as the site of Santa Fe's so-called Tertio-Millennial celebration, promoted by several prominent citizens, including L. Bradford Prince and Arthur Boyle. The grounds were cleared and graded, the stone walls were given a temporary roof, and an exterior stairway was built to the first floor, which was used to house out-of-town Indian participants during the 6 weeks the fair was in progress. They were advertised as practicing crafts and giving chicken pulls, races, tribal dances and other ceremonials, and in one performance the Court House was used as the backdrop for a staged battle between the Indians and Coronado's forces. A racetrack about one-third of a mile long was laid out around the grounds, generally following the present Federal Place oval. Horse, mule and burro races were held here, as were competitive drills by territorial cavalry units.

In May, 1885, a simple stone monument to Kit Carson was erected at the main (south) entrance of the building by his comrades of the Grand Army of the Republic. It was unveiled in the presence of some 5,000 persons from Santa Fe and other parts of New Mexico.

Several more years passed before work started again on the Court House, but it was finally completed in 1889, together with the circular stone wall and iron fence around the federal grounds. An addition at the north, in the same architectural style as the original building, was constructed in 1929-30.

37
RUINS OF FORT MARCY

NORTHEAST OF CITY

ATOP A STEEP HILL overlooking the city of Santa Fe from the northeast within 600 yards of the Plaza lie the remains of Fort Marcy, first United States military post in the Southwest. Although never used, the massive adobe fort symbolized the power of the conquering nation in its expansion of territory to the Pacific Ocean during the Mexican War.

On August 19, 1846, one day after officially accepting the peaceful surrender of New Mexico from Acting Governor Juan Bautista Vigil y Alaríd, Brigadier General Stephen Watts Kearny ordered Lieutenants William H. Emory and Jeremy F. Gilmer to reconnoiter the city to determine the best location for a fort. They selected the obvious location which, as Lieutenant Emory described it, was "the only point which commands the entire town and which itself is commanded by no other." On August 23 work started on the fort, and in a report to Washington, Kearny suggested that it be named for William L. Marcy, secretary of war.

The fort was constructed in an irregular star shape "with adobe walls nine feet high and five feet thick." These walls were surrounded by a ditch 8 feet deep and enclosed an area 270 feet by 80 feet. A log building in the compound was to serve as a powder magazine and a log blockhouse was built east of the gate for additional defense. Barracks, corrals and other facilities were located adjacent to the PALACE OF THE GOVERNORS as they had been under Spain and Mexico.

Inspecting the military facilities of Santa Fe in 1853, Colonel J. K. F. Mansfield wrote: "This is the only real fort in the territory. . . . It is well planned and controls a city of about 1,000 population. The troops do not occupy this fort, but it can be occupied at short notice."

With U.S. authority firmly fixed in New Mexico, Fort Marcy on the hill was neglected and its name came to be applied to the military post which took shape north of the Plaza, ultimately covering the area now bounded by Federal Place and Washington, Palace, and Grant avenues. The 17 acres of land of the old Fort Marcy reservation were transferred to the Department of the Interior in 1891 and sold at public auction to L. Bradford Prince. The ruins of the fort and the land surrounding them were sold to the city of Santa Fe in 1969. The downtown Fort Marcy was abandoned by the army in 1894.

Today, the remains of Fort Marcy on the hill consist of mounds of earth several feet high, tracing the outline of the adobe foundations. The indentations of the ditch are also visible.

38
PINCKNEY R. TULLY HOUSE

136 GRANT AVENUE (PRIVATE RESIDENCE)

THIS ATTRACTIVE 10-room house is an outstanding example of Territorial architecture, and unlike most historic houses in the city, it has undergone no major exterior changes since its original 9 rooms were built in 1851, except for the addition of a tenth room with bay window during the 1880's. The list of its owners and occupants reads like a 19th century *Who's Who* of Santa Fe.

The property on which the house is located was purchased prior to 1851 by James Conklin, a French-Canadian trader who came to Santa Fe in the 1820's shortly after the opening of the Santa Fe Trail. In 1829 he married Juana Ortiz. The previous owner, José Albino Chacón, was a municipal judge and militia officer during the late days of Mexican rule. Conklin's son-in-law, Pinckney R. Tully, also a Santa Fe trader, built the house fronting on "the road from the Plaza to Tesuque" in the summer of 1851. During the middle 1850's the Tully family moved to the Mesilla Valley, and Pinckney was a leading Confederate sympathizer during the Civil War. In 1863 he became a partner of Estevan Ochoa, pioneer freighter in southern Arizona, with headquarters in Tucson.

After Tully left Santa Fe, Conklin mortgaged the property to two other well-known traders: first to William S. Messervy, also secretary of the territory, and then to James T. Webb. In 1857 he deeded the house to another son-in-law, Oliver P. Hovey. Ten years earlier, Hovey had enlisted in Ceran St. Vrain's "mountain men militia company" to assist Colonel Sterling Price in crushing the Taos revolt of 1847. Later that year, Hovey began publication of New Mexico's first English newspaper, *The Santa Fe Republican,* on a press which he had shipped from Missouri. In addition to being a journalist and Indian trader, Hovey was also a member of the territorial legislature. As a staunch Union man at the outbreak of the Civil War, he was commissioned Major General of the Second Regiment of Territorial Militia in 1861. Hovey used the property as security in financial dealings with such controversial men as the ex-priest, José Manuel Gallegos; Alexander M. Jackson, secretary of the territory; and William Pelham, first U.S. surveyor general for New Mexico, who had his office in this house. Both Jackson and Pelham were arrested as Confederates when Union forces reoccupied Santa Fe in April 1862.

Important Santa Feans who owned the property during the late 1800's were Attorney General William Breeden and Dr. Robert H. Longwill, both of whom were members of the "Santa Fe Ring," a group of leading citizens then dominating New Mexican affairs; Rufus J. Palen, long-time president of the First National Bank of Santa Fe; and Henry L. Waldo, chief justice of the supreme court, later solicitor for the Santa Fe Railroad.

During the 20th century, the house was owned by such prominent citizens as Levi A. Hughes, businessman and banker; Mrs. James W. Raynolds, whose husband was at the time secretary of the territory; Miss Grace Bowman, and her partner in the Avery-Bowman Abstract Company, Miss Jennie Avery. Miss Bowman converted a portion of the house into apartments, one of which was occupied in 1926 by New Mexico author Erna Fergusson.

39
ROSARIO CHAPEL & CEMETERY

NORTHWEST OF CITY

THIS CHAPEL WAS GRANTED a building license by the bishop of Durango in 1806 and was completed in 1807. It was intended for the reception of the statue of La Conquistadora during the annual novena, when it was taken in procession from the Santa Fe *parroquia*, now replaced by the CATHEDRAL OF ST. FRANCIS, to the place where General de Vargas, his troops, and colonists were encamped during the reconquest of Santa Fe in 1693. While the soldiers battled the Indians entrenched in the PALACE OF THE GOVERNORS, the women and children prayed for success to the statue of the patroness, La Conquistadora. General de Vargas made a vow to have the procession repeated annually in thanksgiving for the success of his mission. After some lapses, the procession has been held for many years on the first Sunday after the Feast of Corpus Christi, when the statue is taken to Rosario Chapel for a novena of masses and then returned to the Cathedral.

Although de Vargas also vowed to build a sanctuary for the statue, he did not accomplish this. There is no documentary evidence that anything other than a temporary shrine was built at Rosario before 1807, despite the statements of some writers. This date is carved inside the old doorway, and the original corbels and choir loft remain in place. The painted altar screen by Pedro Antonio Fresquís, dated 1809, was planned to contain the statue of La Conquistadora in a central niche into which it fitted nicely. No other image was included; panels were of flowers on a rose field divided by marbleized pillars. Fresquís (1749–1831), born at Santa Cruz, was the first known native New Mexico *santero*. At Our Lady of the Rosary of Las Truchas, he painted another altar screen and several *santos*. The retablo at Rosario Chapel was badly damaged by having wallpaper pasted on it in later years.

By 1914, the chapel was too small for attending crowds, and a large addition was built against the east wall of the nave, which was then opened. This changed the main axis of the chapel from north-south to east-west. The former entrance and sanctuary became transepts. In 1962, a new altar and altar screen were installed, the work of Eugenie Shonnard, a Santa Fe sculptor who studied with Auguste Rodin.

When the CATHEDRAL OF ST. FRANCIS was completed, burials were no longer made in the Cathedral grounds, but at Rosario Cemetery. Many prominent Santa Fe residents, including the late Archbishop Edwin V. Byrne, have been buried there.

40
EL RANCHO VIEJO

TESUQUE, NEW MEXICO (PRIVATE RESIDENCE)

THE ADOBE HOUSE and surrounding land presently owned by Mr. and Mrs. William M. Williams at the northern end of the village of Tesuque, some 6 miles north of Santa Fe, has been known locally for several generations as El Rancho Viejo ("the old ranch"). During the 1830's, it was a portion of the large country estate of Juan Bautista Vigil y Alaríd, important *rico* and politician during the brief period when New Mexico was a part of the Mexican Republic. He was in charge of the treasury in 1825, then first *alcalde* of Santa Fe, and post-

master from 1829 to 1835. Although removed from the offices of treasurer and postmaster for malfeasance, he was nevertheless appointed secretary of government to Manuel Armijo in 1845. In this capacity, it was Vigil y Alaríd's humiliating task, on August 18, 1846, to surrender the capital city of Santa Fe to Brigadier General Stephen Watts Kearny, commander of the U.S. Army of the West, since Armijo had fled south to Mexico.

Vigil y Alaríd was one of the largest landowners in the Santa Fe area during the Mexican period. In the capital, he owned most of the property on the west side of the plaza, including the private chapel of the Holy Trinity. Most of his extensive holdings in the Rio de Tesuque settlement upon which his country hacienda, including still another *oratorio,* was built were acquired from his uncle, Gregorio Alaríd. He purchased the northern portion consisting of El Rancho Viejo, however, in 1838 from Juan Estevan Pino, another powerful *rico* and officeholder under the Mexican regime.

After U.S. occupation, Juan Bautista Vigil y Alaríd took no further part in political affairs. For several years he speculated in dubious land grant claims in the southern part of the territory, and in 1849 liquidated his property in the Tesuque area. El Rancho Viejo, consisting of "a house of four rooms and a piece of farming land," was bought by Doña Peregrina Ortiz who, in turn, sold it to José Dionisio Jiménez.

In 1866, the house and land, which by then contained a sizable orchard, were purchased by Edward Miller, a German-born merchant and pawnbroker living in Santa Fe, and his first wife, Luisa López. Four years later the Millers sold the property, which passed through several hands until 1884 when it again came into the possession of Miller by mortgage foreclosure. In the meantime, his first wife had died and Miller had married Wilhelmina Feivde, also a German immigrant. For many years the Miller family lived on the ranch, which became famous for the excellence of its fruit. When it was sold in 1910, the conveyance described it as "the property commonly known as the Edward Miller Fruit Ranch."

The property was purchased by the present owners in 1941. Minor changes have been made to the original portion of the house, which consists of the living room and three-room northwest wing. Four additional rooms have been added on the south.

41
BOUQUET RANCH

POJOAQUE, NEW MEXICO (PRIVATE RESIDENCE)

THE LAND AND SPRAWLING collection of buildings near the Indian pueblo of Pojoaque known for the past century as "Bouquet Ranch" were part of the country estate of Nicholás Ortiz and his second wife, Josefa Bustamante, when Ortiz was killed by Comanches in 1769. Their property extended for some 2 miles along the north bank of the Nambe River, ending on the west at the road from Santa Fe to Taos. Nicholás' son, Antonio José, inherited the western part, then secured the portion received by his stepmother (who was also his sister-

76

in-law) for satisfaction of debt and purchased additional land on both sides of the river. During the same period, he also enlarged the Santa Fe NICHOLAS ORTIZ III HOUSE to include the portion which bears his name.

When Antonio José made his will in 1805, he divided the lands and "El Rancho de Pujuaque with its two big houses and other small houses in which the servants live" according to the usual Spanish legal custom among his wife, children, and grandchildren whose fathers had died. In her will of 1814, the widow, Rosa Bustamante, made a further partition of her portion. The lion's share of the Pojoaque property, as well as the Santa Fe residence, however, came into the hands of the eldest son, Antonio de Jesús who, in turn, fragmented it among his many heirs by his will of 1837. During the next 30 years, the holdings north of the Nambe River and for a mile east of the Taos road were split up into many small parcels owned by relatives or servants of the Ortiz family.

In 1867, John (or Juan) Bouquet, a Frenchman who had operated a store and wineshop in Santa Fe for several years, began buying land north of the Rio Nambe previously owned by Nicholás, Antonio José, and Antonio de Jesús Ortiz, as well as parcels west of the Taos road. By the time of his death in 1897, Bouquet and his wife, Petra Larragoite, had made two land transfers and purchased 22 pieces of property which contained four houses and a mill built by Antonio de Jesús Ortiz. Among the vendors were various members of the Ortiz family and several Pojoaque Indians.

Bouquet was famous throughout the region for his horticultural talents. He was one of the first farmers in the valley skilled in the technique of grafting to improve the quality of his produce. His large orchard contained many new varieties of fruit trees imported from abroad. He held a government forage contract to furnish hay and grain for the military post in Santa Fe, which he filled from his own excellent crops and those purchased from his neighbors. Whether any of the structures on the property at the time of the Bouquet purchases dates from the original Ortizes is uncertain. The new owner remodeled the existing buildings and constructed others to form a sizable complex which included a general store. Bouquet Ranch was also a stage stop and a hostelry with a reputation for good food.

When Bouquet died in 1897, his widow inherited the ranch. Two years later she married Cicero Weidner who, in 1907, signed an affidavit renouncing all claims to her property. By 1917, the ranch complex had come into the possession of J. H. and Adele B. Crist, but land deeds are silent as to the means by which the well-known attorney and politician acquired the property except for a statement in a later conveyance that he received it for "twenty years of

legal service to the widow Petra L. de Bouquet de Weidner." The Crists received a U.S. patent to 1¼ acres in 1930 as the result of the settlement of the Pojoaque Pueblo Indian land claim by the Pueblo Lands Board. The buildings were further remodeled during their residency.

Bouquet Ranch is presently owned by Mr. and Mrs. Walter L. Goodwin, Jr., who are engaged in its preservation.

77

THE BANDELIER GARDEN OF EL ZAGUAN (TEXT ON PAGE 41)

GLOSSARY

acequia. Irrigation ditch.

acequia madre. "Mother ditch"; main irrigation ditch from which water is diverted into laterals.

alcalde. A municipal official during the Mexican period with authority similar to a justice of the peace.

ayuntamiento. A town council.

baile. Dance or ball.

barrio. Ward or district of a town.

camino. Road.

camino real. "Royal road" maintained at government expense.

casa. House.

casas reales. "Royal houses"; used to identify government buildings.

castrense. Military chapel.

cienega. Area of springs; marshy region.

cofradia. Confraternity; local church society approved by a bishop.

convento. Residence of a Franciscan friar.

estofado. Type of sculpture or painting in which surface is covered with whitewash made of powdered gypsum (*yeso*) and painted. A coat of gold leaf is finally applied. The processes were often executed by different individuals.

fanega. Measure of wheat and other grain equivalent to 1½-2½ bushels.

garita. Sentry box or tower. *La Garita,* north of Santa Fe, was the traditional place of execution during the Mexican period.

genizaros. Indians captured by nomadic tribes who had lost their identity and were captured or ransomed by the Spaniards or wandered into the settlements. They agreed to live in a Europeanized status and settlements were granted to them.

hacienda. Landed property or estate usually containing a sizeable residence.

jacal. Simple dwelling made of wood chinked with adobe.

kiva. Pueblo Indian ceremonial room.

luminarias. Small pitch bonfires lighted for festive occasions.

mayordomo de la acequia. Supervisor of an irrigation ditch or ditch system.

molina. Mill.

muralla. A wall, usually for defensive purposes.

oratorio. Private chapel.

peso. Standard measure of currency considered equivalent of the dollar.

parroquia. A parish church as distinguished from a mission.

placita. A small plaza or square serving a complex of buildings or located in the center of a private home.

plaza. Public square.

plaza mayor. The main town square, situated in the center of a settlement.

politico. Politician.

portal. Long porch or portico with roof supported by vertical posts and corbels.

presidio. Permanent garrison of soldiers.

pretil. Defensive parapet on top of a building; firewall.

rajas. Ax-split pieces of cedar or spruce used for ceilings.

rancho. Small ranch.

reredos. Altar screen.

rico. Rich man.

sala. Reception or drawing room.

santero. A local designer of *santos.*

santo. Image of a saint.

torreon. Defensive tower.

trastero. Hand-carved wooden cupboard.

vara. Measure of distance of approximately 33 inches.

villa. Town or city in Spanish colonial period designated as a center of administration.

vigas. Ceiling beams.

zaguán. Roofed space joining separate buildings or rooms.

79

historic tour of santa fe

KEYED NUMERICALLY TO THE TEXT
SHADED AREA INDICATES THE BARRIO DE ANALCO

SCALE IN FEET 1" = 400'

400 200 0 400 800 1200

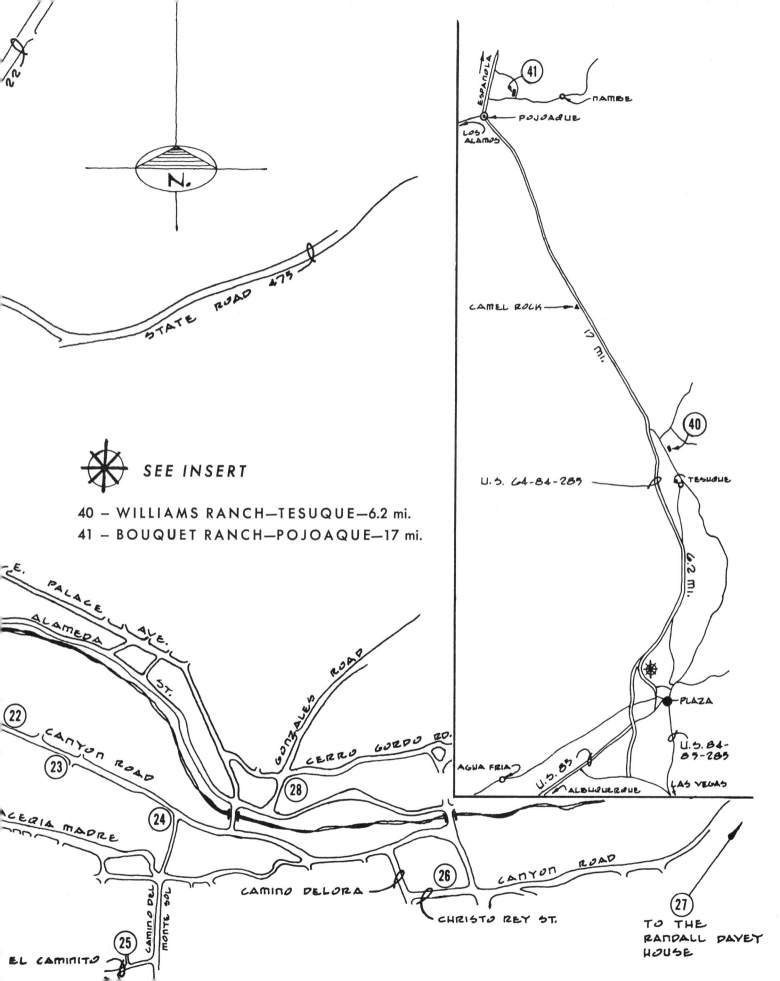

N.

SEE INSERT

40 – WILLIAMS RANCH—TESUQUE—6.2 mi.
41 – BOUQUET RANCH—POJOAQUE—17 mi.

STATE ROAD 475

ESPANOLA

41

NAMBE

POJOAQUE

LOS ALAMOS

CAMEL ROCK

17 mi.

40

U.S. 64-84-285

TESUQUE

6.2 mi.

PLAZA

U.S. 84-85-285

AGUA FRIA

U.S. 85

ALBUQUERQUE

LAS VEGAS

22

E. PALACE AVE.

ALAMEDA ST.

GONZALES ROAD

CERRO GORDO RD.

22

CANYON ROAD

23

28

ACEQIA MADRE

24

CAMINO DEL MONTE SOL

CAMINO DELORA

26

CANYON ROAD

25

EL CAMINITO

CHRISTO REY ST.

27

TO THE RANDALL DAVEY HOUSE